The 'Dispos
the 'Never-P
and the 'Bastards'

Debunking Major's Myths of the Eurosceptics

1990-1997

Luke Stanley

The Bruges Group

The Bruges Group

First Published 2014
by The Bruges Group,
214 Linen Hall, 162-168 Regent Street, London W1B 5TB

http://www.brugesgroup.com/
www.brugesgroup.com

Bretwalda Books
Unit 8, Fir Tree Close, Epsom,
Surrey KT17 3LD
info@BretwaldaBooks.com

ISBN 978-1-910440-04-9

Acknowledgements

First and foremost I should like to thank my supervisor Professor Stuart Ball, whose advice, encouragement and support over the last year made it possible for me to complete this work to its present standard. I offer my sincere appreciation for the learning opportunities Professor Ball has provided me.

This project would also have been greatly diminished without the personal testaments of the political figures I was fortunate enough to interview over the last year: John Redwood; Bill Cash; Peter Lilley and Barry Legg. I am very grateful that they were prepared to take time out of their busy schedules of tending to the country's ailments to be interviewed by an undergraduate.

Lastly I should like to express my gratitude to Robert Oulds, the Director of the Bruges Group. He not only put me in touch with the above interviewees, but gave me the opportunity to put my interest in European affairs to practical use by writing for the Bruges Group.

Contents

List of Figures and Charts

List of Abbreviations

AGM	Annual General Meeting.
EEC	European Economic Community.
EDM-174	Early Day Motion 174 of the 1992-1993 period, 'Future Development of the EEC', proposed by Michael Spicer, 6 June 1992.
EDM-549	Early Day Motion 549 of the 1992-1993 period, 'Fixed Exchange Rates', proposed by Michael Spicer, 24 September 1992.
ERM	Exchange Rate Mechanism.
EU	European Union.
IGC	Inter-Governmental Conference.
MP	Member of Parliament.
NTB	The No Turning Back Group.
NUCUA	National Union of Conservative and Unionist Associations.
OBE	Order of the British Empire.
PM	Prime Minister.
PPS	Parliamentary Private Secretary.
QMV	Qualified Majority Voting.
SEA	Single European Act
WWII	The Second World War.

Introduction

In his memoirs John Major argues that his premiership was damaged by the arrival of a new class of careerist politicians between 1979 and 1992, gradually replacing the 'aldermanic guard' of MPs without ministerial ambitions.[1] In his infamous off-the-record conversation with reporter Michael Brunson, Major labelled three distinct categories of discontented careerists in his party; 'the dispossessed', 'the never-possessed' and 'the bastards'.[2] He believed the 'dispossessed' were angered at their fall from office, 'the never-possessed' at having never been appointed to office with 'the bastards' inside the government coveting his premiership. Major assumed these discontented careerist politicians had concluded that the best way of attacking him was to use the issue of Europe, hoping to precipitate his fall and usher in a government which recognised their talents. To Major, the worst of these careerists were the new 1992 intake of MPs, who were particularly outspoken in their Eurosceptic views in order to establish their Eurosceptic credentials. Together, this thoroughly biased narrative was the official line espoused by Major and his government allies throughout his premiership, up until the present day. As recently as October 2013 Major has described his bastards comment as 'absolutely unforgiveable' with his only excuse being that 'it was true'.[3]

Despite the obvious bias of this hypothesis, with Major and his allies trying to deflect the blame in the aftermath of the Conservative's worst electoral defeat since 1906, this interpretation of the Eurosceptics' motives has found some traction with historians. Seldon argues that Europe was used as a way of 'bashing down the leader they held in contempt', whilst Hugo Young states that the rebel's 'real passion was for deconstructing John Major'.[4] Bale agrees that in the 1992 intake, MPs such as Iain Duncan Smith and Bernard Jenkin, being 'skilful troublemakers'

---

1 J. Major, *The Autobiography* (St. Ives, 1999), p. 347.

2 *The Times*, 26 July 1993, p. 1.

3 *Huffington Post*, 22 October 2013.

4 A. Seldon, *Major: A Political Life* (Guernsey, 1998), p. 522; H. Young, *This Blessed Plot: Britain and Europe from Churchill to Blair* (London, 1998), p. 396.

would better serve their careers than 'a few years anonymity'.[5] Whilst Seldon and Young's interpretations can be excused by their writing in the immediate aftermath of the defeat, Bale's recent interpretation demonstrates the endurance of this strain of thought within the historiography of the period. This is understandable. Not only is the period relatively recent, but the controversy around Britain's relationship with the EU still dominates the current political climate, and seems likely to do so for the foreseeable future. The recentness of the period has restricted the number of academic accounts on the subject, whilst its ongoing nature has impaired the impartiality of many accounts. Indeed, the majority of sources on this topic are primary sources, either written by the Eurosceptics themselves, their opponents in government or the equally biased press. The primary purpose of this work is therefore to act as an unbiased revision of the subject, to prove that the allure of climbing the Greasy Pole was not the dominant reason behind most Eurosceptics' behaviour.

Moreover, understanding the reason why certain Eurosceptics were more rebellious than others in their opposition to Major's pragmatic approach to Europe is becoming more important than ever. With the Prime Minister's proposed renegotiation and referendum on EU membership set to take place in 2017 recognising the factors affecting MPs' willingness to defy the party line is vital. Should Cameron secure re-election at the head of a minority or slim-majority government, the ensuing Europe debate within the Conservative Party is likely to be even more divisive than Maastricht. Understanding MPs' behaviour on Europe will allow the pro-withdrawal faction to assess the optimum methods of convincing MPs to side with them, as well as how to counter the Europhile faction's attempts to poach their followers. The secondary purpose of this work is therefore to act as a case study for newer Eurosceptic MPs to study. This will ensure that, unlike the Maastricht rebellion, the Eurosceptics will have an advantage. Lastly I hope to show that those Eurosceptic backbenchers who voted against the government and those frontbenchers that resigned over their convictions achieved far more than their colleagues who did not do the same.

---

5 T. Bale, *The Conservative Party: From Thatcher to Cameron* (Cambridge, 2010), p. 43.

Chapter One

The Aldermanic Guard departs

On 31st October 1990 Margaret Thatcher infamously proclaimed her opposition to further European integration to the Commons, precipitating the resignation of Geoffrey Howe and the leadership challenge from Michael Heseltine. During the first ballot, Thatcher failed by four votes to win the contest outright, after which her remaining support began to drain away. Two days later, on 22nd November 1990, she withdrew her candidature, allowing Major to enter the contest in order to prevent a Heseltine victory, which he duly did, becoming Party Leader and Prime Minister on 27th November.

Since Ted Heath led the UK into the EEC in 1973, defeating the Anti-Marketeer rebels from both parties, Euroscepticism had become a muted opinion. The majority of Conservative Anti-Marketeers had reconciled themselves to the realpolitik situation that Britain leaving the EU was out of the question. This is best demonstrated by John Biffen, a leading Anti-Marketeer in the 1970s, guiding European legislation (the SEA) through Parliament in 1986. However, following Thatcher's Bruges Speech in 1988 which denounced the idea of further integration, Conservative Party Euroscepticism was undergoing a gradual revival. Thatcher's growing Euroscepticism is also demonstrated by her reluctance to join the ERM, a system fixing exchange rates between EEC currencies to foster convergence ahead of a common currency. Thatcher agreed to join the system in 1990, following Chancellor Nigel Lawson's resignation over the issue and the advice of his replacement, Major. This Eurosceptic revival remained muted however, giving the deceptive impression that the movement was still confined to the fringes within the Party when Major came to power, with Seldon likening it to 'hidden icebergs of opposition'.[6]

---

6 Seldon, *Major*, p. 166.

In the immediate aftermath of the Leadership Election, both the Right and the Left were pleased with the result. As Dorey argues, because Major was a pragmatist, he was 'claimed as "one of us" by the left and right "wings" of the Party'.[7] Very few Eurosceptics realised that Major was far from Eurosceptic, at least until his Bonn Speech in March 1991 when Major declared the UK must be 'at the very heart of Europe'.[8] John Redwood was one MP who did recognise Major's Euroagnosticism, with Redwood attempting to persuade Norman Tebbit to stand in the Leadership Election.[9]

In January 1991 there was an attempt to set up a group of elder statesmen to preserve Thatcherism, including opposition to further European integration, from the backbenches, which its co-founder Nicholas Ridley referred to as the Steering Wheel Group. The idea was that the elder statesmen; Thatcher, Tebbit, Ridley and Cecil Parkinson would act as inner circle, whilst Michael Spicer would act as a co-ordinator drawing in newer MPs and Tebbit, initially a supporter of Major, would act as a bridge to the Prime Minister. Other MPs involved included George Gardiner, Bill Cash and Robert Jones. The group's success was limited however. Tebbit had partially retired in order to tend to his injured wife after the Brighton bombing whilst Ridley was ill, dying in March 1993. By November 1991, Spicer was writing that it was time that these elder statesmen gave way as they were ditherers.[10] The Steering Wheel Group had unravelled by the time its four elder statesmen retired to the Lords in 1992.

But to what extent was the Steering Wheel Group motivated by loss of office frustration? Tebbit had resigned for his wife, Parkinson resigned when Thatcher left and Ridley had been forced to resign by his own political incorrectness. This leaves only Thatcher and Spicer open to the accusation of anger at dismissal. Spicer writes that on 25 November 1990, he told Major's campaign team he 'would not expect to be a member' of Major's government, should he win due to differences regarding the ERM, which would appear as a face-saving tactic.[11] Indeed, Gove wrote that Spicer was 'sacked', not that he resigned.[12] Spicer was a recalcitrant

---

7 P. Dorey (ed.), *The Major Premiership* (Basingstoke, 1999), p. xiii.

8 Seldon, *Major*, p. 167.

9 J. Redwood, *Singing the Blues* (London, 2004), p. 115.

10 M. Spicer, *The Spicer Diaries* (London, 2012), 8, 21 January, 15, 16 April and 17 November 1991, pp. 177-191.

11 *Ibid.*, Reflections, p. 172.

12 M. Gove, *Michael Portillo: The Future of the Right* (London, 1995), p. 194.

rebel who went on to spearhead the Maastricht Rebellion, and therefore he may be one of the few Eurosceptics motivated by dismissal. Thatcher's Euroscepticism was prominent before her ousting, as demonstrated by the Bruges Speech. It is possible her dismissal hardened her Euroscepticism, with Young claiming her attitude towards Major was 'classic hatred for a usurping son'.[13] However, Thatcher could have been a much more difficult ex-premier had she wished to be, much as Heath had been to her. Instead she kept a low profile throughout the remainder of the 1987 Parliament. Indeed she only spoke out against Maastricht in December 1991, later claiming that she couldn't sit by while Britain's 'status as a sovereign state, was at issue', before retiring to the Lords.[14] Had her intent been to cause as much trouble as possible she would have remained in the Commons as Heath had done.

Between 9th and 10th December 1991, Major attended the Maastricht IGC, negotiating changes to the Treaty of Rome, with other EEC leaders. There were two key policy areas that concerned Major; securing opt-outs for the UK from the Single Currency and the Social Chapter. The former would allow Britain to retain the pound sterling, if it decided to, whilst other countries adopted a common currency. The latter would exempt Britain from regulations concerned with employment policy, which Conservative MPs vehemently opposed. Going into the negotiations there were discussions between Eurosceptic members of the government as to what their course of action should be if Major failed to secure these two opt-outs. Peter Lilley, Secretary of State for Trade and Industry, states that Junior Ministers in the government were willing to resign if he and other Cabinet Ministers did. Lilley himself considered resigning over Maastricht but was concerned he might set off a series of other resignations, bringing down the government and allowing in a Labour government. However, had the opt-outs not been secured on the Single Currency and the Social Chapter, Lilley would have resigned, as a Labour government's Maastricht agreement could have been no worse.[15] Meanwhile, Ridley and Tebbit both attempted to persuade Junior Ministers Edward Leigh and Michael Forsyth to resign, according to Spicer, but were unsuccessful.[16]

The opt-out from the Single Currency was obtained easily, with Major having secured German Chancellor Kohl's support earlier in the year. The second was

---

13 *Guardian*, 6 June 1995, p. 4.

14 M. Thatcher, *The Path to Power* (London, 1995), p. 475.

15 Interview with Peter Lilley MP, 21 January 2014.

16 Spicer, *Diaries*, 10 December 1991, p. 193.

trickier, only being secured on the last day of the conference, after much wrangling by Major and Lamont. Indeed during the conference, Major phoned Michael Howard, Secretary of State for Employment, who was the greatest opponent of the Social Chapter within the government, asking him if he would accept a watered-down version, to which Howard refused. Privately, he made it known he would have to consider resigning if Major failed to secure the concession.[17] However, Major did secure both objectives and the Commons endorsed these terms on 19 December 1991. Only seven Conservatives voted against the terms, with three abstentions, the former including Tebbit and Biffen, and Thatcher the latter.[18]

Whilst this result did much to reassure Major that the Conservative Party supported his pragmatic approach to the EU, he was aware that Cabinet Ministers had considered resigning, and that there were opponents to the legislation on the backbenches. In 1991 Cash was offered a PPS job at the Foreign Office, being told that he would have a great future if he accepted, but that if he refused he would not be offered anything again.[19] Tim Renton, a Chief Whip during Thatcher's government later lamented that he should have recommended Cash for a position as Junior Minister to Thatcher, before his Euroscepticism could harden.[20] Similarly outspoken Eurosceptic James Cran was also offered a PPS in December 1991 but he refused the position saying he couldn't consider it until Maastricht was over.[21] For these two Eurosceptics, jobs were certainly not as important as their convictions.

As we have seen, aside from a few isolated resignation threats and a handful of rebellious votes, Eurosceptic criticism was very limited during the Maastricht negotiation. Seldon convincingly argues that Eurosceptic opposition was, 'masked by the need for Party unity, and respect for Major as new leader after November 1990', both of which had waned by May 1992.[22] The new Parliament was to be drastically more outspoken in its criticism of Major and his Euroagnosticism. Dr. Heppell's work on the 1992 Parliament includes a categorisation of each Conservative MP into

---

17 Seldon, *Major*, p. 247.

18 http://hansard.millbanksystems.com/commons/1991/dec/19/maastricht [accessed 5 May 2014].

19 Interview with Bill Cash MP, 17 December 2013.

20 T. Renton, *The Chief Whip: People, Power and Patronage in Westminster* (Croydon, 2005), p. 319.

21 C. Gill, *Whip's Nightmare: Diary of a Maastricht Rebel* (Spennymoor, 2003), p. 40.

22 Seldon, *Major*, p. 295.

the categories of those who favoured 'interdependence' with Europe (Europhiles), 'independence' from Europe (Eurosceptics) and 'European policy agnostics' (Euroagnostics). He identifies 98 MPs as Europhile, 41 as Euroagnostic and 192 as Eurosceptic, with 5 MPs without sufficient data to judge. When this data is used in conjunction with other statistics about Conservative MPs of the 1992 Parliament, factors that correlate to these three views on Europe can be identified, and a causal relationship can be hypothesised on (see Appendix II. Unless stated otherwise, all Figures and Tables are based on this data).

Table 1.1. Gender and Europe Convictions of Conservative MPs in 1992.

Europe Conviction	Male	Female	TOTAL
Europhile	93 (29.7%)	5 (27.8%)	98 (29.6%)
Euroagnostic	41 (13.1%)	0 (0.00%)	41(12.4%)
Eurosceptic	179 (57.2%)	13 (72.2%)	192 (58.0%)

Table 1.1 shows that there is a slight correlation between gender and Europe conviction, with female Conservative MPs more likely to be Eurosceptics instead of Euroagnostics, but their percentage of Europhiles are almost the same as that as the percentage of Europhiles in the Party as a whole. The conclusion this implies is that if female MPs didn't like Europe, they really didn't like Europe. However, 18 Female MPs is hardly a large enough sample to be statistically reliable and McAllister's research shows that, 31% of Conservative female candidates in the 1997 General Election were Eurosceptic, compared with 45% of men.[23] As such no correlation between gender and Europe conviction can be reached.

However, the age of MPs do appear to correlate with their European convictions; with the later the year of the MP's birth, the more likely they are to be Eurosceptic. This is likely due to these younger MPs growing up during the Thatcher years, leading them to support her policies, growing steadily more Eurosceptic along with her during the 1980s. Young supports this hypothesis stating that 'a time lag' had produced 'a Thatcherized party only after the heroine had gone'.[24] Ridley's

23 I. McAllister and D. Studlar, 'Conservative Euroscepticism and the Referendum Party in the 1997 British General Election', *Party Politics*, 6, no. 3 (2000), p. 363.

24 Young, *Plot*, p. 396.

assertion in 1992 that Young Conservatives were 'uneasy' about the drift towards federal union supports this notion.[25] Older MPs can be understood to be in favour of greater European integration, in order to prevent another European War, having either grown up in the shadow of, or fought in as Ted Heath did, WWII. This trend is further reinforced by Figure II, which demonstrates that, allowing for some fluctuation, the later the Conservative MPs entered Parliament, the more likely they were to be Eurosceptic.

Table 1.2 Constituency Nature and Europe Convictions of Conservative MPs in 1992.

Europe Conviction	Borough	County	TOTAL
Europhile	39 (30.7%)	59 (28.9%)	98 (29.6%)
Euroagnostic	14 (11.0%)	27 (13.2%)	41(12.4%)
Eurosceptic	74 (58.3%)	118 (57.8%)	192 (58.0%)

Constituency concerns also correlate with the Eurosceptic convictions of their MPs, as Figures III, IV and V demonstrate. Figure III demonstrates that Eurosceptic MPs' were more likely to have constituencies in the Midlands or the North, whilst Europhiles were more likely to have constituencies in the South or Wales, and Euroagnostics in Scotland. This could have multiple explanations. Firstly, the populations of Scotland, Wales and the South could be more pro-European than the population of the Midlands and the North, explaining why MPs in these areas would espouse Europe views similar to those of their constituents. Secondly, variations in the number of borough and county constituencies across these regions could explain the correlation. Lastly, the correlation could simply be random and not a causal link. Whilst there is more support for European integration in Wales and Scotland today, in the 1975 referendum, a larger percentage of the population of England voted to stay in the EEC than in Scotland and Wales. Moreover, polls are also unrepresentative of the total population's convictions. This leaves the first explanation unverifiable. The second is disproved by Table 1.2, which shows there is almost no variation between Europhiles, Euroagnostics and Eurosceptics in

25 N. Ridley, *My Style of Government: The Thatcher Years* (London, 1992), p. 228.

Borough and County constituencies. As such there is no conclusive explanation for the regional constituency distribution of each Europe grouping.

Figure IV demonstrates that there is a correlation between Europe conviction and constituency majority, with Europhiles and Euroagnostics more common in safer seats. Again, there is no case to be made for a causal link between constituency majority and Europe conviction, but it should be borne in mind for Chapter Two. Finally, Figure V demonstrates the enduring legacy of former Eurosceptic MPs on their constituencies. The chart shows that, if the constituencies which were abolished between 1971 and 1992 and the constituencies held in 1992 by an opposition party are discounted, 71.4% of constituencies held by Anti-Marketeer Conservatives in 1971 are still held by Eurosceptic Conservatives in 1992. Here the causal link is obvious. As Crowson argues, constituency associations with a history of Eurosceptic MPs have already been 'indoctrinated with the sceptical argument'.[26] These Eurosceptic associations then either selected candidates who shared their Europe convictions or their new MPs felt compelled to act Eurosceptic in order to appease their constituency associations.

To recap then, there were 192 Eurosceptics (58.0% of Conservative MPs) in the Conservative Party from May 1992. Their Eurosceptic views were influenced by age, parliamentary experience, constituency history, and perhaps also by their gender, constituency location and majority, as well as their personal convictions. Unfortunately, Major's Cabinet did not represent the composition of this new Parliament as Figure VI demonstrates, with a far larger percentage of Europhiles in his Cabinet than in the Parliamentary Party as a whole. Not only were there fewer Eurosceptics than there should have been, they held less senior posts. With the exceptions of Lamont 1992-3 and Howard 1993-1997, the four high offices were dominated by Europhiles and Euroagnostics; Major, Ken Clark and Douglas Hurd throughout the period, with Heseltine wielding greater influence than the office of the President of the Board of Trade should have entitled him, before becoming Deputy Prime Minister in 1995. The composition of the government was therefore vastly out of touch with its backbenchers' convictions on Europe, and while the number of Eurosceptics in Cabinet increased throughout the period, the 'Euro-enthusiastic' wing 'always retained their majority in the Cabinet'.[27] This coupled

---

[26] N. J. Crowson, *The Conservative Party and European Integration Since 1945* (Abingdon, 2007), p. 167.

[27] J. W. Young, *Britain and European Unity, 1945-1999* (Basingstoke, 2000), p. 169.

with the fact that the majority had fallen to just 21 meant that the rebellious Eurosceptic backbenchers had both a motive and a means to effectively oppose the PM's pragmatist policies on Europe.

The backbenchers were also becoming more organised in forming groups to press their policies, Forster arguing these groups 'reflected a growing determination of MPs to be autonomous from their political parties in obtaining and disseminating information.'[28] Longstanding organisations like the 92 Group became indoctrinated by Eurosceptic arguments with its Chairman Gardiner stating that it consisted of 'nearly a hundred backbenchers' including both hard-line Eurosceptics and Major loyalists.[29] Major argued that he abused his position as chairman to present his own views as the views of the group to the government, demonstrating how powerful these organised backbench groups could be.[30] The No Turning Back Group, founded to pursue Thatcherite policies, was another Eurosceptic organisation, consisting of backbenchers such as Iain Duncan Smith and Barry Legg, as well as Cabinet and Junior Ministers including Michael Portillo, Lilley, Leigh, Redwood, Forsyth and Neil Hamilton. This group was more effective in mobilising opinion than the 92 Group, the majority of which sided with the government during the Maastricht Rebellion.

The passage of the Maastricht Treaty through the Commons began on 1 May 1992, with the Second Reading of the Bill. There were 22 Conservative rebels during the vote, a marked rise from the seven in December the previous year. This rise can be explained by the increased proportion to Eurosceptics in the Party and their growing boldness due to the slim majority. On 3 June 1992 the Danish rejected the terms of the Maastricht Treaty in a referendum which in the words of Seldon, acted as a further 'catalyst' for the hardening of Eurosceptic opinions within the party.[31]

The following day Spicer introduced EDM-174, calling for a Fresh Start on Europe policy, which received 81 signatures, discounting the three signatures withdrawn. Gardiner claims that whips threatened the new intake with denying

---

28 A. Forster, 'Anti-Europeans, Anti-Marketeers and Eurosceptics: The Evolution and Influence of Labour and Conservative Opposition to Europe', *The Political Quarterly*, 73, no. 3 (2002), p. 304.

29 G. Gardiner, *A Bastard's Tale: The Political Memoirs of George Gardiner* (London, 1999), p.16

30 Major, *Autobiography*, p. 357.

31 Seldon, *Major*, p. 295.

them promotion if they did not withdraw their names.[32] Meanwhile, Major argues that Cash tricked many new MPs to sign the EDM, which is inconsistent with the fact only two backbenchers retracted their signatures.[33] David Evans, as a PPS was not allowed to support EDMs and Olga Maitland and Hartley Booth presumably bowed to whip pressure. Following the EDM Nicholas Winterton, Peter Fry, Harry Greenway and Ivan Lawrence all lost their Select Committee positions, with a new rule being introduced barring MPs serving for more than 3 Parliaments from being eligible to sit on Select Committees.[34] Whilst the timing of this rule is likely coincidence, the 1992 entrants who had signed the EDM; Jenkin, John Whittingdale, David Lidington, Alan Duncan and Charles Hendry received no Select Committee positions, whilst Maitland and Booth both did.[35]

Out of EDM-174, the Fresh Start Group evolved, a group of around twenty MPs led by Spicer, with membership fluctuating throughout the period. Baker summarises their plan as trying to delay ratification of the Maastricht Bill for as long as possible, whilst also pushing for a referendum and amending the Treaty until it was ruined.[36] Lynch rightly argues that Maastricht was successful in bringing together Eurosceptics of different factions within the Fresh Start Group, 'providing a sense of common purpose'.[37] However, the effect of the Fresh Start Group on the number of rebel votes is easily overstated. As Fresh Starter Legg argues, the majority of the group 'were strong individuals that worked out their positions for themselves'.[38] As such they would likely have voted against Maastricht whether they were a member of the group or not.

The effect on the Eurosceptics in government was similar to the effect on the backbenchers. Resignation considerations begun anew, with Eurosceptic Ministers meeting the same day to discuss what could be done about Maastricht.[39] Eurosceptic

---

32 Gardiner, *Bastard's*, p. 11.

33 Major, *Autobiography*, p. 349.

34 *The Times*, 10 July 1992, p. 9.

35 *Ibid.*, p. 14.

36 D. Baker, A. Gamble, and S. Ludlum, 'The Parliamentary Siege of Maastricht 1993: Conservative Divisions and British Ratification', *Parliamentary Affairs*, 47, no. 1 (1994), p. 38.

37 P. Lynch, *The Politics of Nationhood: Sovereignity, Britishness and Conservative Politics* (Chippenham, 1999), p. 95.

38 Interview with Barry Legg, 20 December 2013.

39 *The Times*, 9 June 1992, p. 8.

whip David Davis was there, making it unlikely that resignation would have been discussed openly. However, at a NTB meeting later that same month Leigh said outright that the Treaty needed to be abandoned.[40] Leigh was the minister who seemed to consider resigning most seriously but, according to Teresa Gorman, he was persuaded that his resignation would achieve nothing by Portillo, Redwood and Lilley.[41] Redwood himself had already considered resignation but had concluded that his case could be better made from within the government.[42]

A further catalyst was to deepen the Eurosceptic fervour with both the backbenches and the government on 16th September 1992. After several months under pressure from currency speculators, the Bank of England was forced to hike up interest rates in an attempt to stave off devaluation. This would have led to the Pound's value falling relative to the Deutschmark below the threshold allowed by the ERM, thus ejecting Britain from the mechanism. After several hours of sustained pressure, Major was forced to devalue and exit the mechanism having wasted billions of the Bank of England's reserves. 16th September 1992, also known as Black Wednesday ruined Major's reputation, as well as the Conservative's economic reputation. Most importantly however, it solidified the feeling that further integration in Europe was to be resisted. Redwood was in the process of writing his resignation letter over continued membership of the ERM when the Pound was forced out, whilst the Chancellor Norman Lamont remarked to Lilley the next day, 'now we've got the policy we've always wanted'.[43] This demonstrates the depth of Euroscepticism in the government in the wake of Black Wednesday. Meanwhile, many Eurosceptic backbenchers were overjoyed that their suspicions about Europe had been proven correct and that Britain was out of the ERM, referring to the day afterwards as White or Golden Wednesday. Some such as Rhodes Boyson were unsurprised however, later writing that ERM was like 'a twelve-legged race in which twelve people had their legs tied together and were then made to run. Of course they all fell down'.[44]

---

40 Gove, *Portillo*, p. 255.

41 T. Gorman, *The Bastards: Dirty Tricks and the Challenge to Europe* (London. 1993), p. 169.

42 Interview with John Redwood MP, 10 December 2013.

43 Redwood, *Blues*, p. 122; Lilley interview.

44 R. Boyson, *Speaking My Mind* (London, 1995), p. 234.

Chapter Two

'Emotional rivers burst their banks'[45]

These are the words which Major used to describe the effects of Black Wednesday on the Eurosceptic convictions of Conservative MPs. In the wake of Black Wednesday, Major temporarily suspended the passage of the Maastricht legislation, before holding a Paving Vote on whether to continue the committee stage of the bill on 4th November 1992. Following a narrow victory of three votes, the committee stage of the bill was resumed, passing its Third Reading on 20th May 1993. The hardening of Eurosceptic MPs' stances is demonstrated by the number of rebel votes rising from 22 in the Second Reading to 32 in the Paving Vote, before reaching 41 in the Third Reading. A total of 43 Conservative MPs voted against the Maastricht Bill in either the Second Reading, the Paving Vote or the Third Reading. Whilst this is a substantial number, it falls far short of Heppell's estimate of 158 Eurosceptic backbenchers. Closer scrutiny of the factors that affected voting behaviour is therefore required.

The first aspect to consider is the varying degrees of Euroscepticism within the Party. As Bale asserts, the strength of convictions held by 'Eurosceptic "true believers" meant they were able to resist' the government's whipping operations.[46] This contrasts starkly with the accredited Eurosceptic Jill Knight, who agreed that whilst it was 'entirely right that Britain's sovereignty … be safeguarded', Maastricht did not threaten this.[47] Similarly some Eurosceptics, such as Michael Fabricant, sympathised with the rebels cause, but not their methods due to the effects on the Party.[48]

---

45 Major, *Autobiography*, p. 352.

46 Bale, *Party*, p. 52.

47 J. Knight, *About the House* (London, 1995), p. 208.

48 Major, *Autobiography*, p. 374.

A commonly-peddled theory is that the rebellion was led by what Heseltine described as the 'Once-Promoted-Now-Demoted' wing of the Party, insinuating that the rebellion was, at least partially, revenge based.[49] However, this hypothesis does not stand up to scrutiny. Only seven of the 43 rebels were ex-ministers, not including one ex-PPS. Of these eight, three (Taylor, Walker and Knapman) had all resigned their posts in opposition to their respective governments' European policy. Budgen, had similarly resigned over his convictions, in this case regarding Northern Ireland whilst Biffen was an anti-Marketeer during Britain's entry into the EEC, long before taking office. This leaves only three rebel MPs, Boyson, Butcher and Spicer, with only Spicer being dismissed by Major, as previously discussed. As such, only one of the 43 rebels could be motivated by anger at dismissal. Heseltine's 'Once-Promoted-Now-Demoted' MPs can therefore be better described as being 'Once-Promoted-Now-Retired'.

One of the factors that did affect the rebel vote was the support of Eurosceptic elder statesmen for the rebels' position. Lord Tebbit had demonstrated his continued ability to command support with his barnstorming anti-Maastricht speech at the 1992 Conservative Conference. On the night of the Paving Vote, Tebbit sat in the members' lobby to encourage wavering Eurosceptics to vote against the bill. Thatcher also met with MPs, particularly the new intake, around the time of the Paving Vote in order to encourage those wavering. Indeed, it is believed she reprimanded Whittingdale for his intention to abstain by commenting that his spine evidently did not reach his brain. However, it is easy to overstate Thatcher's involvement in the rebellion. As we have seen, in Cash's words Thatcher was 'sensitive to her position as a former Prime Minister' and, as such, the Maastricht Rebellion was not 'by any means a coordinated approach' between her and the Eurosceptic backbenchers.[50] Another prominent figure that acted to shore up rebels' resolves was Enoch Powell, who sent letters of congratulation to Gill regarding his anti-Maastricht position. Powell continued to advise Gill on methods to resist European integration up until his death.[51]

Career patronage is a key factor to consider when analysing the pro-Maastricht Eurosceptic vote. Whilst, as we have seen, Eurosceptic MPs in the 1992 Parliament tended to be younger in age and have less parliamentary experience than Europhiles

---

49 M. Heseltine, *Life in the Jungle: My Autobiography* (London, 2000), p. 518.

50 Cash interview.

51 Gill, *Nightmare*, pp. 62, 122-3, 182.

Table 2.1 Average Years of First Entry by Frequency of Rebellion

Frequency of Rebel Votes	Average Year of First Entry
1	1982.3
2	1978.4
3	1975.3

and Euroagnostics, Figures VII and VIII demonstrate that the majority of Eurosceptic rebels were older and had been in Parliament longer than loyalists. Indeed, almost half of the Eurosceptic loyalists entered Parliament between 1987 and 1992. This is further compounded by Table 2.1 which demonstrates that if we consider the MPs who rebelled once, twice or all three times out of the three selected votes, the more rebellious ones had more parliamentary experience, with all 6 rebels of the 1992 intake rebelling only once. Gill argues, this was an attempt to keep 'future options open', which is likely to be one aspect newer Eurosceptics considered.[52] Furthermore, 15 MPs who signed EDM-174 welcoming the Danish Referendum result in 1992, publically declared on the day of the Paving Vote, that following the ERM exit 'events in Europe are moving to meet our own views', rendering rebellion over Maastricht unnecessary.[53] All 15 were 1992 entrants. Amongst the 1992 intake there were MPs, such as Barry Legg, who asserted that 'the stakes were just too high' to be concerned about future parliamentary careers, but these were in the minority.[54] One Eurosceptic MP, Hartley Booth, was made a PPS mere days after the Paving Vote.[55] Whilst this endorses Major's assertion that many new MPs were career politicians, it is clear that the rebels were the enduring 'aldermanics' and the loyalists the careerists rather than the other way around.

However, it was not only the 1992 intake who were tempted with patronage. Robert Jones, a longstanding Eurosceptic backbencher and member of the Fresh Start Group, was made a Junior Minister within a year of his voting with the government over the Paving Vote. Despite this, most longstanding backbenchers were less likely to be tempted by careerist considerations as they realised they were

---

52 *Ibid.*, p. 76.

53 N. Waterson et al, *The Times* (4 November 1992).

54 Legg interview.

55 *Guardian*, 18 November 1992, p. 7.

too old to enjoy successful government careers. For example, Sir Peter Tapsell, a Eurosceptic who had entered Parliament in 1959, ignored Heseltine's advice that he vote with the government as it would be better for his career prospects.[56] Instead, longstanding backbenchers were tempted by honours rather than careers. In 1991, Taylor voted with the government over Maastricht, later admitting to taking the 'Queen's shilling', to get his knighthood.[57] During the vote on the Social Chapter in June 1993, Gyles Brandreth records that Nicholas Winterton voted with the government, according to another MP, because he was 'frantic for a knighthood ... and our excellent Whips probably promised him one'.[58] Therefore, whilst newer backbenchers were more likely to side with the government to safeguard their career prospects, some older Eurosceptics were prepared to vote against their consciences more occasionally in order to gain honours, before then returning to the rebel fold.

Blackmail and intimidation, particularly threats 'to expose extra-marital conduct by backbench colleagues' were tactics that whips were prepared to use to persuade Eurosceptics to vote with the government.[59] As Baker points out however, these stick tactics were only used when carrot ones had failed.[60] Of course, successful use of blackmail is not well documented and can only be speculated about. However, examples of intimidation are more widely recorded. For example, whips Andrew Mitchell and James Arbuthnot both attempted to pressure Jenkin into voting with the government during the Paving Vote by harassing his wife with phone calls.[61] Bill Walker was threatened with losing his chairmanship of the Scottish Affairs Committee over his stance on the Paving Vote whilst whip Lennox-Boyd threatened Michael Clark with having his trip to Canada rescinded.[62] Furthermore, during the Paving Vote itself, Gill claims that Greenway was 'physically manhandled into the Government lobby' by the whips.[63] Most shocking of all is Teresa Gorman's

---

56 Gorman, *Bastards*, pp. 148-149.

57 *Ibid.*, pp. 144-145.

58 G. Brandreth, *Breaking the Code: Westminster Diaries May 1990-May 1997* (London, 1999), p. 194.

59 N. Fairbairn, *The Times*, 10 November 1992, p. 17.

60 D. Baker, A. Gamble and S. Ludlam, 'Whips or Scorpions? The Maastricht Vote and the Conservative Party', *Parliamentary Affairs*, 46, no. 2 (1993), p. 153

61 Gorman, *Bastards*, pp. 124, 128.

62 *Ibid.*, p. 116; Baker, 'Scorpions', p. 157.

63 Gill, *Nightmare*, p. 61.

assertion that two unnamed Conservative MPs sexually intimidated her on the day of the Paving Vote.[64] Incontrovertibly, there was a whip spy within the Fresh Start group who reported to the government; Major admitting that notes on Fresh Start meetings were left anonymously on a desk in the Whip's Office, although he didn't know the spy's identity.[65] Whilst, the Fresh Starters each had their own ideas as to the who the informant was, his identity was never confirmed for certain.

Major threatened a dissolution of Parliament and a general election should he be defeated over the Paving Vote. This might be the most crucial explanation for why so many accredited Eurosceptics voted with the government. It was widely accepted that any general election would inevitably bring in a Labour government, which would be far more pro-European integration than Major himself. This was the argument that Gardiner, Townend, Pawsey, Dunn and Boyson used when they wrote to the Telegraph on the day of the Paving Vote, urging Eurosceptics to side with the government.[66] Moreover, as Figure X demonstrates, 38% of Eurosceptic loyalists had majorities of less than 10%, compared with the 16% of Eurosceptic rebels. Evidently fears that a government defeat would precipitate a general election made some Eurosceptics anxious they would lose their seats.

Whip involvement in constituency associations were another method used to encourage wayward Eurosceptics to vote with the government, with a constituency visit by a central office official or a call from a whip usually being followed up with that constituency's association urging their MP to side with the government. Examples of this tactic range from Sweeney's constituency of Glamorgan to Budgen's constituency of Wolverhampton South West.[67] The Chairman of the NUCUA's Executive Committee, Basil Feldman, also urged MPs to support the Paving Vote, writing that Conservative activists had not worked hard to secure victory for their MPs so they could vote with Labour.[68] However, this tactic was not always successful. Norman Fowler noted that a whip's 'gauche attempt' to pressure Fry through his constituency did not help his own attempts to win him over.[69] Indeed,

---

64 Gorman, *Bastards*, p. 132.

65 Major, *Autobiography*, p. 373.

66 Boyson, *Speaking*, p. 230.

67 Crowson, p. 174; Gorman, *Bastards*, p. 117.

68 B. Feldman, *The Times*, 4 November 1992.

69 N. Fowler, *A Political Suicide: The Conservatives' voyage into the wilderness* (London, 2008), p. 152.

many associations actively supported their MPs Maastricht stance, examples being Cash and Redwood's constituencies.[70] Figure IX shows that all Eurosceptics' with constituencies in the North supported the government whilst ones in the Midlands were more likely to rebel, perhaps being a result of association opinion differing between regions. Overall, the majority of Eurosceptics' constituencies, such as Christopher Gill's, were divided between party loyalty and conviction, Spicer arguing the party loyalists were office holders, whilst the rank and file were Eurosceptic, much like in Parliament.[71]

Fowler's attempt on Fry was not an isolated phenomenon of frontbench MPs being used to influence Eurosceptic's voting behaviour. Redwood argues that Eurosceptic Ministers had 'an especial duty to argue and persuade Euro-sceptic colleagues of the need to vote for the legislation', although he himself was not utilised, nor was Lamont who had volunteered.[72] Lilley recalls he 'was assigned one or two people to talk to', in order to persuade them to vote with the government which he attempted by pointing out if the government fell Labour would be far worse.[73] The majority of this work was performed by less outspoken Eurosceptics, perhaps explaining Major's reluctance to use Redwood or Lamont. Examples of these 'accredited Eurosceptics' as Williams describes them, were Howard, Davis and Heathcoat-Amory, both of which were mobilised as the face of relaxed Euroscepticism in order to reassure Eurosceptic backbenchers that the government shared their concerns.[74] The role of accredited Eurosceptics in persuading the soft-Eurosceptics to side with the government cannot be overstated, perfectly complimenting the whip's role in pressuring the hardliners. However, even as some Eurosceptic Ministers were convincing backbenchers to side with the government, others were still considering their own positions.

As seen in Chapter One, resignations had already been discussed, both during the Maastricht negotiation and in the aftermath of the Danish referendum. In the wake of Black Wednesday however, the Eurosceptics in government began to seriously consider whether to resign, as they came under increasing pressure from

---

70 Cash interview; Redwood interview.

71 Gill, *Nightmare*, p. 54; Spicer, *Diaries*, 20 March 1993, p. 218.

72 Redwood, *Blues*, p. 128; N. Lamont, *In Office* (London, 1999), p. 328.

73 Lilley interview.

74 H. Williams, *Guilty Men: Conservative Decline and Fall, 1992-1997* (London, 1998), pp. 35, 40.

backbenchers to act on their convictions. At a No Turning Back meeting days before the Paving Vote, Lord Harris urged the members of government at the meeting to leave at once for Downing Street as a group and tell Major to withdraw the motion.[75] This request was naturally ignored, but Major records in his memoirs that Portillo, Leigh, Eric Forth and Peter Lloyd attempted to see him during the passage of Maastricht, he believes, to threaten to resign. However, after Major made it clear he would see them one at a time, and that he would be accepting their resignations, they backed down.[76] Leigh later admitted that there had been discussions of mass resignations. However, he said the PPSs wanted to resign, but only would if the Junior Ministers did, who in turn wanted the Cabinet Ministers to resign with them.[77]

However, the Cabinet Ministers were reluctant to resign. As recorded earlier Redwood wanted to make his case from within the government whilst Lilley did not want to bring down the government. In the aftermath of Black Wednesday Major's standing was crippled and never recovered, allowing leadership speculation to run rampant throughout the rest of his premiership. On the Right, both Howard and Portillo were perceived as Major's potential successors, whilst Heseltine and Clarke were seen as heirs apparent on the Left. As such neither Howard nor Portillo were eager to leave the Cabinet, familiar with how Heseltine's influence had waned after his resignation from Thatcher's Cabinet. Spicer, eager to play the kingmaker, wrote as early as December 1991 of the need to build up Howard and Portillo to defeat Heseltine when Major goes whilst sustaining Major until they were ready.[78]

Some Junior Eurosceptic Ministers were also eager to stay within the government. As seen above, Major made good use of Eurosceptic ministers such as Davis and Heathcoat-Amory during the Maastricht rebellion. For many, their promotion prospects remained tied to Major's success, in particular Davis who had jumped on the Major bandwagon whilst Ministers such as Portillo, Leigh and Forsyth were still trying to convince Thatcher to stand for a second ballot. Williams argues that 'non-threatening Euroscepticism ... explained the elevation of David Davis and William Hague to positions just below the Cabinet' in 1994.[79] Heathcoat-Amory

---

75 Legg interview.

76 Major, *Autobiography*, p. 372.

77 Gove, *Portillo*, p. 258.

78 Spicer, *Diaries*, 14 December 1991, p. 195.

79 Williams, *Guilty*, p. 69.

also perceived his promotion to the Treasury in 1994 as due to his Eurosceptic links with the Fresh Start Group which could prevent their rebellion over the EU Budget.[80] Similarly Spicer wrote in May 1992 that Cranbourne had made a deal with Major, to be made Leader of the Lords if he remained loyal over Maastricht.[81]

In hindsight two ministers, Chancellor Norman Lamont and Junior Minister Leigh, might as well have resigned over Europe, both being sacked on 27th May 1993, a week after Maastricht passed its Third Reading. Major told Leigh that he needed a 'united team', and because of Leigh being a conviction politician, as demonstrated by his Maastricht stance, he could not be part of that team.[82] However, Brandreth's assessment that Leigh was being, 'too pushy and too openly disloyal', is a more accurate description.[83] Lamont's forced resignation was far less kind however, with Major offering Lamont the demotion to the Department of Environment, which Lamont refused. The cruel part of the resignation is that following Black Wednesday, Major had told Lamont not to resign as he did not believe Lamont was to blame. Indeed it was Major who had convinced Thatcher to join the Mechanism. Conversely, Lamont did not approve of Britain's membership of the ERM, but had accepted it when he became Chancellor in 1990. Major's motive in telling Lamont not to resign in September and then effectively dismissing him in May was to use Lamont as a scapegoat to deflect blame from himself. Even Seldon concedes that in the aftermath of Black Wednesday, 'if Lamont went, it would make his own position more vulnerable'.[84]

---

80 D. Heathcoat-Amory, *Confessions of a Eurosceptic* (Croydon, 2012), p. 57.

81 Spicer, *Diaries*, 5 May 1992, p. 209.

82 *The Times*, 28 May 1993, p. 3.

83 Brandreth, *Code*, p. 177.

84 Seldon, *Major*, p. 319.

Chapter Three

Turkey's voting for Christmas

After the rebels failed to halt Maastricht in the Third Reading, the consensus between the different groups of Eurosceptic evaporated. Although Maastricht had passed its Third Reading, the Commons still had to vote on an amendment reintroducing the Social Chapter to the treaty. The rebels divided between those who wanted to vote with Labour in favour of the Social Chapter in order to wreck the Treaty, and those who had given up trying to prevent Maastricht's passage. In the event, Major lost one of the votes on the Social Chapter, and forced another vote as part of a confidence motion, which if he lost an election would be called. This succeeded in forcing all but one absenter to vote with Major, finally concluding the Treaty's ratification on 23 July 1993. The lack of cohesion in the Eurosceptic ranks, again divided by faction and also now by their preferred Eurosceptic leadership candidate, prevented a common aim being pursued by the Eurosceptics. As such, 1993-1997 can be perceived as a period of hiatus in the Party, with the Eurosceptics achieving very little. The internal divisions only intensified during the approach to the 1997 General Election. As it became clear that Major was doomed, the leadership posturing of candidates for his replacement proceeded apace.

Although the Maastricht rebellion ended, reprisals against the rebels carried out both by local constituency associations and the government continued. One of the more infamous Eurosceptics, Gardiner's constituency attempted to oust him as their candidate at the next election on several occasions. In July 1993, one of his association committee members faxed him a letter calling on him and the other rebels to 'resign their seats to make way for Conservative candidates' who would support Major.[85]

[85] Gardiner, *Bastard's*, pp. 220-221.

In April 1994, Gardiner was then informed by his constituency chairman that she thought he should retire at the next general election. Gardiner was able to survive for several years by enlisting the begrudging support of Number 10 after informing them he would resign his seat if he was deselected, thereby reducing the majority. Central Office's support for Gardiner expired in January 1997 when he described Major as Clarke's ventriloquist dummy, and he was deselected by the association later that month.[86]

Legg and Cash were two MPs who suffered similar attempted oustings, but survived them, both of these led by the government. Legg's Association Chairman, a known opponent of his stance on Europe, was invited to Downing Street to have tea with the Prime Minister, after which she began attempts to undermine Legg's position in the constituency. After failing to deselect Legg at the constituency's AGM in 1995, the Chairman resigned and within two months was granted an OBE.[87] Cash's attempted ousting was during a boundary review of his constituency in 1996. During the review a Central Office official informed Cash he was not the guaranteed candidate of the new constituency, and that he had no greater right than any other member of the public, despite this being the case for all incumbent MPs during boundary reviews. However, overwhelming support for Cash within the constituency association led to his being adopted as the candidate in any case.[88]

Whilst Redwood was undoubtedly the most high profile resignation of the period, there was a group of ministers who either resigned or threatened to. In November 1994, Party Vice-Chairman Patrick Nicholls was forced to resign, following his comments to constituents that he wasn't comfortable in the EU, due to it being dominated by France and Germany.[89] In 1996, Cran resigned as PPS to the Northern Ireland Office, to concentrate on retaining his seat.[90] However, neither of these examples demonstrates the growth in convictions of Eurosceptic Ministers. In February 1995 Charles Wardle, a Junior Minister at the Home Office resigned over fears concerning the potential scale of internal EU immigration. Whilst at first this would appear a principled stand, further scrutiny shows that this was merely Wardle's pretext for his own discontent working for Howard, as Williams

---

86 *Ibid.*, pp. 220-6.

87 Legg interview.

88 Cash interview.

89 Brandreth, *Code*, p. 284.

90 *The Times*, 8 October 1996, p. 8.

argues.[91] Their relationship had become strained during work over Ali Fayed's citizenship application.[92] A journalist also questioned whether Wardle's resignation was due to his being moved sideways instead of promoted in the previous reshuffle.[93] Either way, Wardle's resignation appears far from a principled Eurosceptic stand. The most senior resignation, aside from Redwood's, was the resignation of Heathcoat-Amory, who had reached the office of Paymaster General. On 16th May 1996, Heathcoat-Amory met with Major to announce his resignation over Major's decision not to rule out Britain's adopting of the Single Currency. Williams cynically claims his resignation only occurred 'once he realised that he was not going to become a Cabinet Minister' and 'was an attempt to display former convictions'.[94] This interpretation is reinforced by an anonymous friend of Heathcoat-Amory, who in *The Times* claimed he 'could not see the point of continuing as a middle ranking minister' and used the Single Currency issue as a way out.[95]

Major's position continued to deteriorate after Black Wednesday, with three Eurosceptic backbenchers separately calling for his resignation in March 1994 after he failed to prevent changes in the QMV system in the Council of Ministers.[96] As a leadership challenge became more inevitable, on 22nd June 1995, Major resigned as Party Leader to flush out his opposition within the Party and regain his reputation. The question was less would someone stand from the Eurosceptic wing of the Party than who would stand?

With Portillo perceived as the champion of the Right, it could be assumed that Portillo would act as the challenger. However, the extent to which Portillo was eager to challenge Major has often been overstated. Firstly, as Gove points out, Portillo's speeches were meant to establish himself as a serious politician, not undermine Major. He was not necessarily to blame for inevitably becoming, 'a dauphin for the discontented'.[97] Indeed in 1993 Redwood offered Portillo his support when the time came for a leadership election, whilst Gardiner promised him the support of the 92 Group 'when the time came', also setting up a secret campaign headquarters and

---

91 Williams, *Guilty*, p. 73.

92 M. Crick, *In Search of Michael Howard* (London, 2005), p. 350.

93 *The Times*, 13 February 1995, p. 1.

94 Williams, *Guilty*, p. 40.

95 *The Times*, 23 July 1996, p. 2.

96 Seldon, *Major*, pp. 453, 455.

97 Gove, *Portillo*, p. 236.

team in case Major should leave office suddenly.[98] This is not to suggest that Portillo was a mere figurehead with no ambitions of his own. He was surely aware, as Spicer was, that in a Leadership Election against Heseltine, he would either become Prime Minister or Heseltine's deputy, benefiting whatever the outcome.[99] Despite this, Major took Portillo by surprise with his announcement, and Gove said he did not think it sensible to run against Major at a time of his choosing.[100] Furthermore, his 'addiction to the inside track' also made him cautious of doing anything to jeopardise his position. Indeed, the installations of Portillo's infamous telephone lines, a pre-emptive measure ahead of a potential second ballot, were actually installed without his knowledge by his political advisor.[101]

Lamont was already preparing to mount a leadership challenge in the autumn, to act as a stalking horse. As such he was a candidate to mount a challenge following Major's resignation. He did attempt to secure support for his bid, but had limited success, eventually agreeing to stand aside for Redwood when the time came. It is incontrovertible that Lamont was motivated out of anger at his dismissal from office. However, it is an injustice to claim as Williams has that Lamont's Euroscepticism was merely, 'a political mechanism designed to eject the Prime Minister', given that Lamont was a Eurosceptic whilst he was in government.[102] Much as with Thatcher and Spicer, Lamont's dismissal, in the words of Gove, only added an 'edge of relish to his attacks' and was already, 'a sceptic to his sinews' when in government.[103] Another potential candidate was Lilley who's candidature was 'certainly discussed on the grounds that ... somebody who could maximise the vote' should be the challenger, if there was to be one, rather than a stalking horse. Ultimately, as Redwood decided to resign and run himself, his candidature meant that Lilley's resignation was not necessary.[104]

As seen in earlier chapters, Redwood had been tempted to resign for some time but ultimately he decided to do so 'when it became apparent that the leadership of the Party was in doubt about using the opt-out' from the Single Currency secured at

---

98 Seldon, *Major*, p. 438; Gardiner, *Bastard's*, pp. 30, 34.

99 Spicer, *Diaries*, 2 May 1994, p. 25.

100 Gove, *Portillo*, p. 319.

101 *Ibid.*, p. 294.

102 Williams, *Guilty*, p. 254.

103 Gove, *Portillo*, p. 233.

104 Lilley interview.

Maastricht.[105] On 16th June 1995, Redwood informed Major that he was resigning to stand. Interestingly Redwood approached Portillo, offering to run as his second if he decided to resign and join him. Portillo refused however, for the reasons already discussed, but he did tell Redwood he expected him to stand aside for him in the event of a second ballot which he could stand for, to which Redwood in turn refused.

The ballot of the leadership election, described by *The Sun* as Redwood versus Deadwood, took place on 4th July 1995, with Major winning by 129 votes.[106] Despite this clear victory, 89 MPs voted for Redwood and 14 abstained, which totals almost a third of the Parliamentary Party. As such the reasoning behind this voting behaviour merits attention. Unfortunately, due to the secret ballot nature of the contest, research as rigorous as over Maastricht is impossible, with data only available for MPs who declared their voting intentions

Predictably, Major levels the charge of careerism at Gorman and Gill, both of whom sided with Redwood and were, according to Major, desperate to become ministers, despite having no chance.[107] This theory is supported by Williams, at least in regard to Gill who was the only Redwood supporter in 1995 to ask him what job he should expect if Redwood won.[108] Careerism does not explain the supporting of Redwood by MPs who had previously demonstrated they cared little about their own, such as Legg and Cash. Another possibility is low constituency majorities of Redwood supporters. As Bale states, Thatcher's fall 'showed that a government in trouble could be rescued from the abyss by a swift change at the top'.[109] Spicer concurs with this interpretation, in part at least, writing that Redwood supporter Thomas Arnold, with a 1.7% majority, viewed the contest as 'a question of who will save his seat'.[110]

Major supporters were not driven by any purer motives however. Spicer's knighthood in 1996 can be regarded as a reward for his heavy involvement in Major's camp. Likewise, Williams maintains that Baker sided with Major as 'he had his eye on a peerage', which he duly received.[111] As Crick points out, with Hurd retiring as

---

105 Redwood interview.

106 *Independent*, 27 June 1995.

107 Major, *Autobiography*, p. 354.

108 Williams, *Guilty*, p. 104.

109 *Bale*, Party, p. 48.

110 Spicer, *Diaries*, 27 June, p. 295.

111 Williams, *Guilty*, p. 111.

Foreign Secretary, it 'was a good time to be loyal'.[112] This could explain why Howard, 'pressed to be included' in Major's team, whilst Davis predictably involved himself, manning telephones for Major.[113] Lang also records that Forsyth involved himself in Major's team, knowing that if Lang were promoted, he would get Lang's job at the Scottish Office.[114] Constituency opinion also affected voting behaviour, with Lang arguing that after Thatcher's ousting, association chairmen 'were not going to have another leader shot out from under them'.[115]

Of the elder statesmen, Thatcher supported Major as she didn't believe Portillo was ready, whilst Tebbit and Powell both endorsed Redwood. Portillo's followers, such as Duncan, Jenkin and Whittingdale, feared that Heseltine would win a second ballot and so they supported Major. They also feared that if Redwood was successful he would supersede Portillo as heir apparent to the Right of the Party. In the end this split in the Right cost Redwood the election, but Portillo's failure to stand and the gaffe over his telephone lines leads Spicer to conclude that Portillo is 'out of the race'.[116] After the Leadership Election there were attempts to foster peace between Redwood and Portillo ahead of Major's inevitable general election defeat. This failed but was irrelevant following the "Portillo moment", in 1997 when he lost his constituency.[117]

---

112 Crick, *Howard*, p. 319.

113 I. Lang, *Blue Remembered Years: A Political Memoir* (London, 2002), p. 217; S. Hogg and J. Hill. *Too Close to Call: Power and Politics - John Major in No. 10* (St. Ives, 1995), p. 272.

114 Lang, *Blue*, p. 221.

115 Interview with Lang, quoted in Seldon, *Major*, p. 577.

116 Spicer, *Diaries*, 4 July 1995, p. 327.

117 Williams, *Guilty*, p. 160.

Conclusion

To conclude it is clear that, for the most part, the Eurosceptic rebels were motivated by their consciences more than their careers. Their voting behaviour was also affected by their ages and parliamentary experience, with younger, less experienced MPs tending to be Eurosceptic, but of these the older, more experienced ones were more likely to be rebellious. A few staunch Eurosceptics were dissuaded from voting against the government by stick initiatives, whilst a few were tempted away by carrot incentives. I hope I have sufficiently highlighted the likely tactics of the whips in order for all true conviction politicians to be prepared for the avalanche of sustained pressure from the government in the next Parliament over all matters European.

It is true that the attacks of some Eurosceptic rebels, such as Thatcher, Lamont, Leigh and Spicer, were made more callous by bitterness, but this does not detract from the convictions behind their actions. As such Major's notion that the Eurosceptics rebellion was primarily motivated by personal dislike for him can be dismissed as nonsense. The Eurosceptics were Eurosceptics because of their strength of convictions on Europe. Whilst Major often bemoaned that some Eurosceptics 'cared less about Europe than about removing me from office', he seemed incapable of grasping the concept that removing him from office would be the best way to get the policies they wanted.[118] His portrayal of the whole Maastricht affair as a personal vendetta against himself, as well as a careerist crusade by Eurosceptic rebels, is a true epitaph to a Prime Minister who worried far too much about what others thought of him.

Indeed, in characteristic Major style, he was right in that Parliament had been infiltrated by career politicians, with the 'aldermanic guard' of MPs without ministerial ambition on the retreat, but wrong about their identity. The true Eurosceptic careerists were those junior ministers such as Davis and Heathcoat-Amory, who were so instrumental in intimidating the MPs that shared their own convictions to vote against those shared convictions. Similarly the majority of Eurosceptics in the 92 intake, such as Fox, were clear careerists. Perhaps

---

118 Major, *Autobiography*, p. 352.

the accredited Eurosceptics in the junior branches of the government and the backbenches subscribed to the Greasy Pole rationale, thinking that they need only follow the orders of their higher ups until they themselves were in a position to pursue their own Europe policies. However, the careers of most of these Eurosceptic loyalists have all but ended, with Davis and Fox on the backbenches, Heathcoat-Amory out of Parliament and Hague retiring in 2015. As such the purpose, if they did intend to change Britain's relationship with the EU when they were in power, of their plans have failed massively.

Conversely, as Redwood states, 'the one thing that came out of that leadership contest ... was that Mr. Major did then promise that we would not enter the Euro without a referendum', with Mr. Blair afterwards having to 'match the offer'.[119] As such, his resignation and loss in the Leadership Election in 1995 was a victory. Similarly successful in their aims were the Eurosceptic backbench rebels themselves. On 20 August 1993 Tapsell sent a letter to Spicer assuring him that, although they had lost the Maastricht rebellion, their actions meant that, 'no Conservative government in our political lifetime will attempt to venture any further down the path towards a European union'.[120] As such the aftermath of the Maastricht rebellion still affects us today, and seems set to do so for the foreseeable future. This is a fitting testament to those MPs that were prepared to sacrifice their careers in the attempt to keep the United Kingdom a sovereign nation. Hopefully the 'Dispossessed', the 'Never Possessed' and the 'Bastards' of Maastricht will inspire future generations of conviction politicians, as equally as they have me.

119 Redwood interview.

120 Spicer, *Diaries*, 20 August 1993, pp. 235-236.

Appendix I – Figures[121]

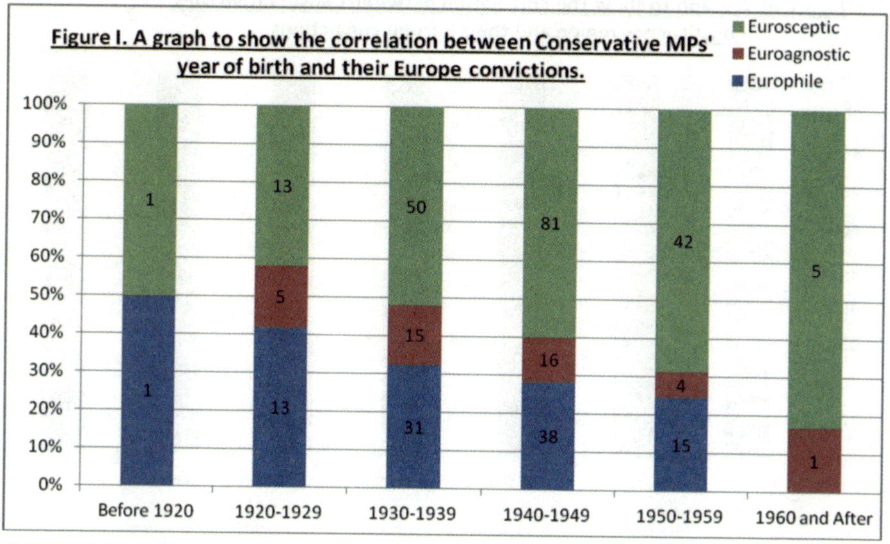

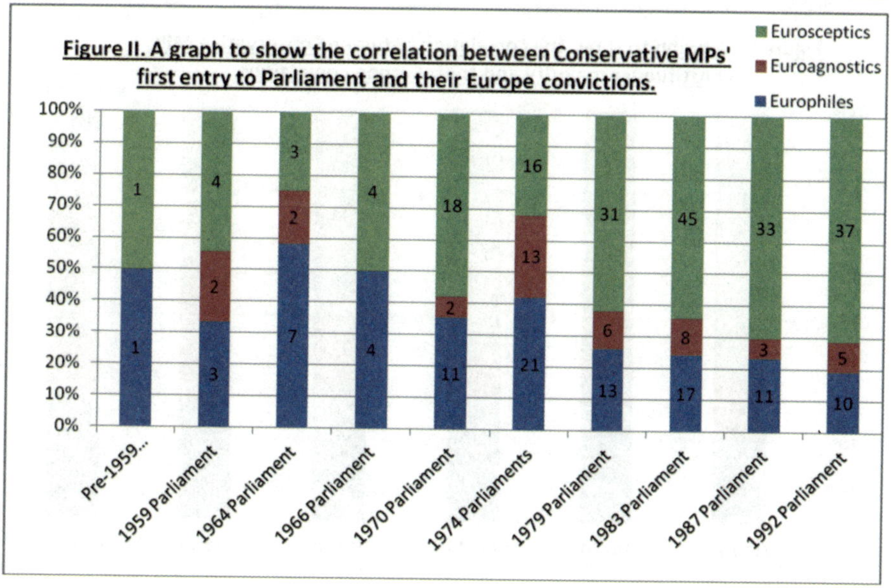

121 All Figures based on data in Appendix II.

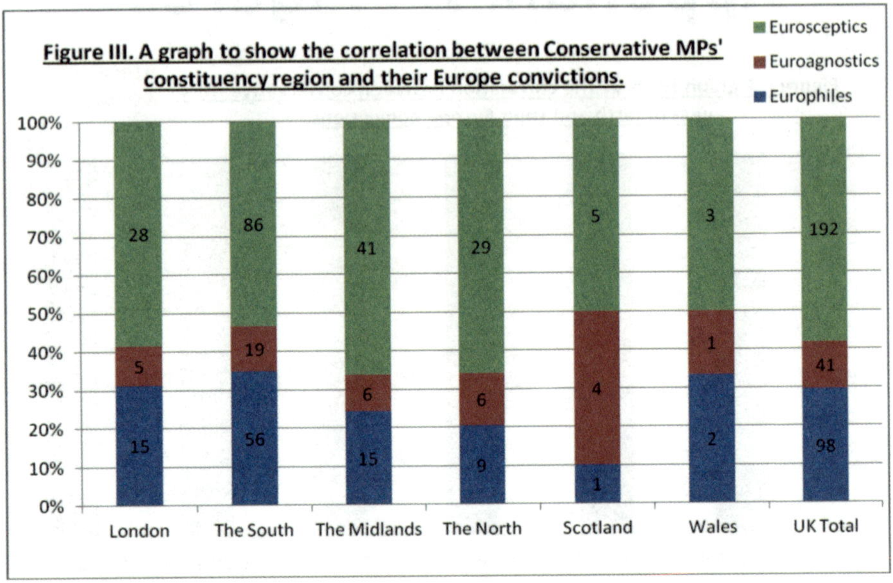

Figure III. A graph to show the correlation between Conservative MPs' constituency region and their Europe convictions.

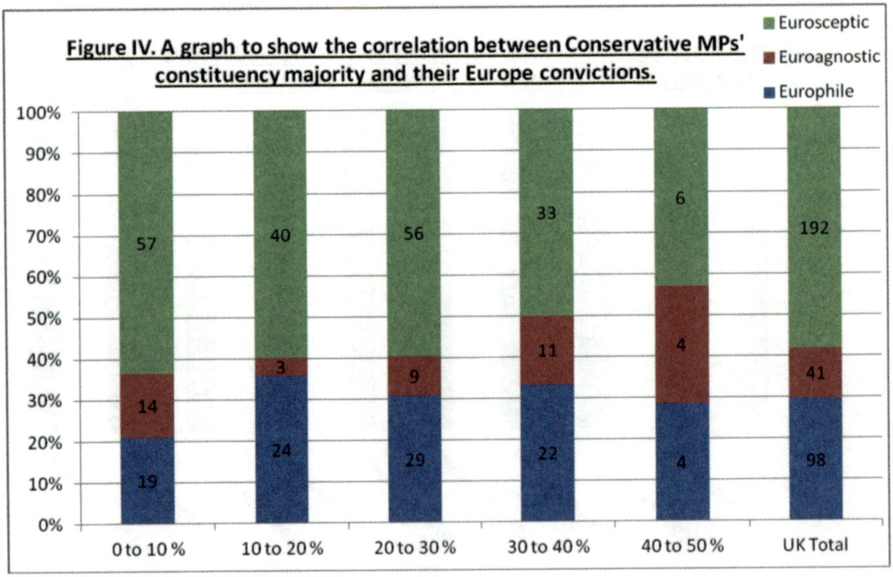

Figure IV. A graph to show the correlation between Conservative MPs' constituency majority and their Europe convictions.

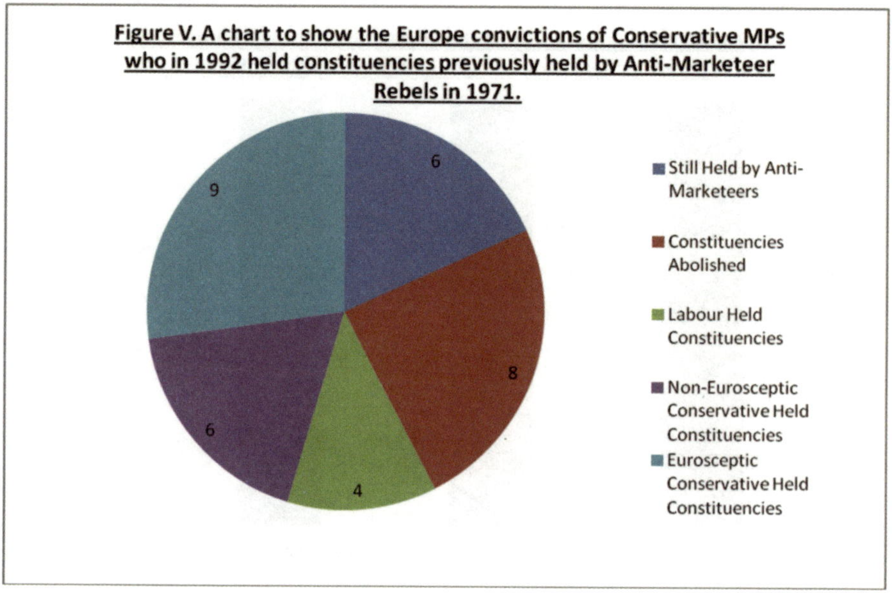

Figure V. A chart to show the Europe convictions of Conservative MPs who in 1992 held constituencies previously held by Anti-Marketeer Rebels in 1971.

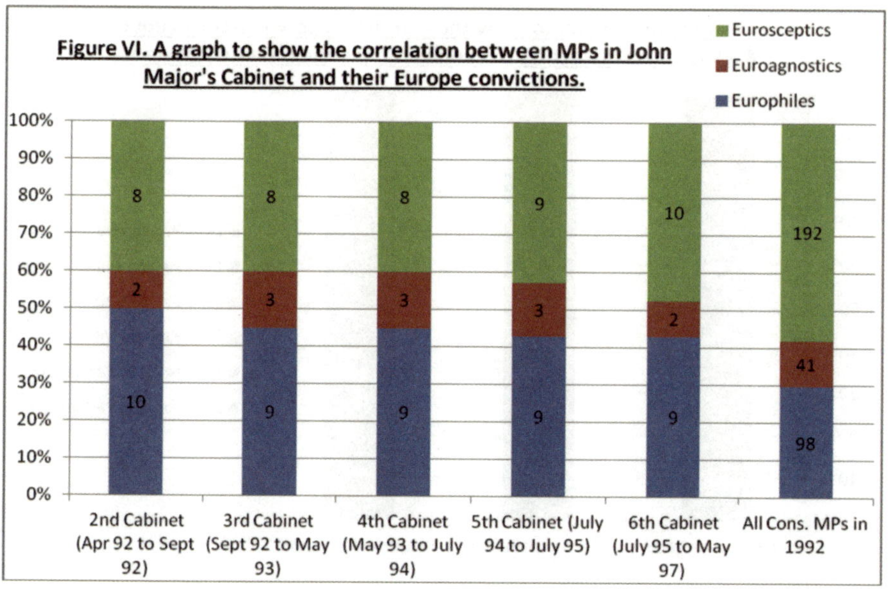

Figure VI. A graph to show the correlation between MPs in John Major's Cabinet and their Europe convictions.

Figure VII. A graph to show the correlation between Eurosceptic Backbenchers' year of birth and their Maastricht stance.

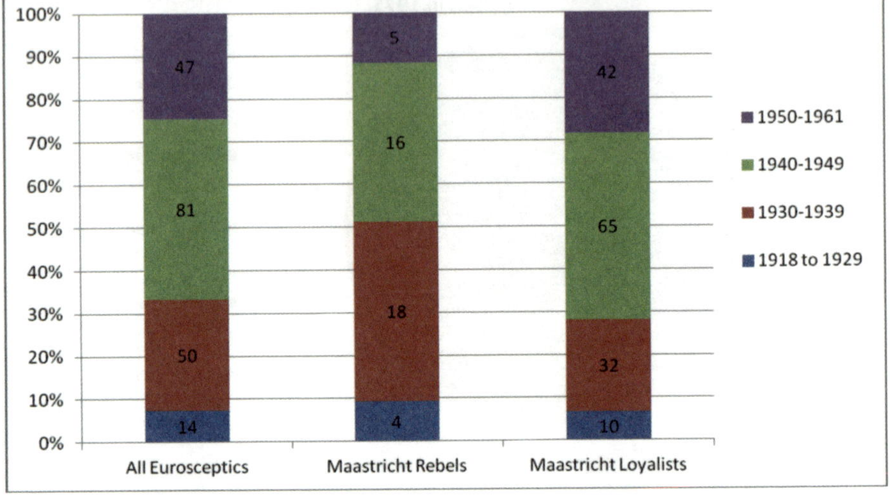

Figure VIII. A graph to show the correlation between Eurosceptic Backbenchers' first entry to Parliament and their Maastricht stance.

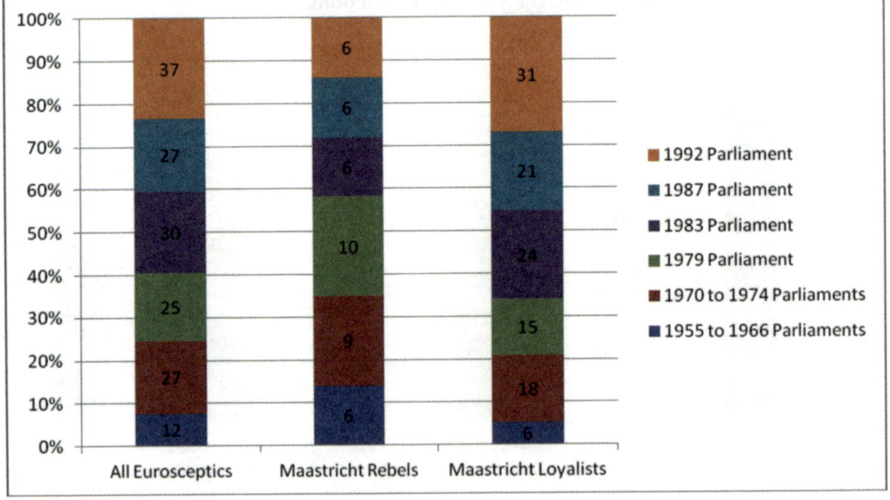

Figure IX. A graph to show the correlation between Eurosceptic Backbenchers' constituency region and their Maastricht stance.

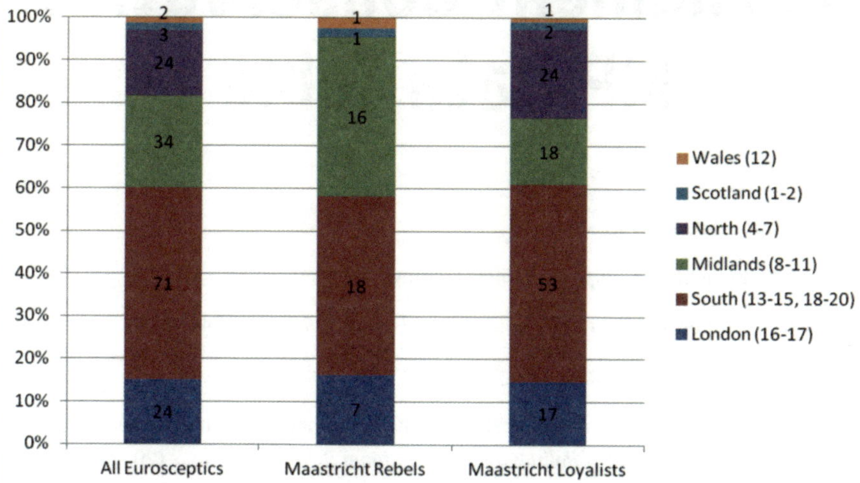

Figure X. A graph to show the correlation between Eurosceptic Backbenchers' constituency majority and their Maastricht stance.

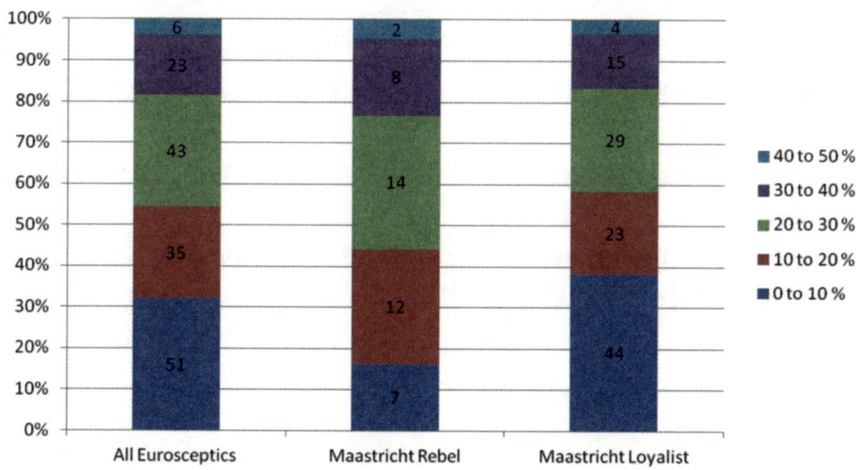

Appendix II – 1992 Parliament Conservative MP Data Table[122]

[121] Data from the following sources:

Dod's Parliamentary Companion 1993 (Etchingham, 1993);

D. and G. Butler (eds.), *British Political Facts* (London, 2011), pp. 44-47;

Gill, *Nightmare*, pp. 230-231;

T. Heppell, 'The ideological composition of the Parliamentary Conservative Party 1992-97', *British Journal of Politics and International Relations*, 4, no. 2 (2002), pp. 299-324;

C. Rallings and M. Trasher (eds.), *British Parliamentary Election Results 1983-1997* (Aldershot, 1999);

http://www.electoralcalculus.co.uk/regional_defns.html;

http://hansard.millbanksystems.com/commons/1992/may/21/european-communities-amendment-bill;

http://hansard.millbanksystems.com/commons/1992/nov/04/european-communities-amendment-bill;

http://hansard.millbanksystems.com/commons/1993/may/20/european-communities-amendment-bill [accessed 31 January 2014].

Surname	Forenane	Heppell's Europe Groupings	Gender	Birth	First Entry	Position 1 May 1992 to 20 May 1993	Constituency	Region	Nature	Majority (%)	EDM-174 Signatories	EDM-549 Signatories	Maastricht Rebel?	Number of Rebellions
Alison	Michael	Euroagnostic	M	1926	1964	Backbencher	Selby	Northern England	County	15.4	Non-Signatory	Non-Signatory	Loyalist	N/A
Ashby	David	Euroagnostic	M	1940	1983	Backbencher	Leicestershire NW	Middle England	County	1.6	Non-Signatory	Non-Signatory	Loyalist	N/A
Aspinwall	Jack	Euroagnostic	M	1933	1979	Backbencher	Wansdyke	Southern England	County	20.5	Non-Signatory	Non-Signatory	Loyalist	N/A
Baker	Nicholas	Euroagnostic	M	1938	1979	Member of Government	Dorset N	Southern England	County	16.1	Non-Signatory	Non-Signatory	Loyalist	N/A
Banks	Robert	Euroagnostic	M	1937	1974	Backbencher	Harrogate	Northern England	Borough	21.2	Non-Signatory	Non-Signatory	Loyalist	N/A
Bates	Michael	Euroagnostic	M	1961	1992	Backbencher	Langbaurgh	Northern England	County	2.4	Non-Signatory	Non-Signatory	Loyalist	N/A
Brooke	Peter, Hon.	Euroagnostic	M	1934	1977	Member of Government	City of London & Westminster South	London	Borough	38.5	Non-Signatory	Non-Signatory	Loyalist	N/A
Bruce	Ian	Euroagnostic	M	1947	1987	Backbencher	Dorset S	Southern England	Borough	23.2	Non-Signatory	Non-Signatory	Loyalist	N/A
Burns	Simon	Euroagnostic	M	1952	1987	Backbencher	Chelmsford	Southern England	Borough	25.9	Non-Signatory	Non-Signatory	Loyalist	N/A
Channon	Paul	Euroagnostic	M	1935	1959	Backbencher	Southend W	Southern England	Borough	23.8	Non-Signatory	Non-Signatory	Loyalist	N/A
Clappison	James	Euroagnostic	M	1956	1992	Backbencher	Hertsmere	Southern England	County	33.1	Non-Signatory	Non-Signatory	Loyalist	N/A
Douglas-Hamilton	James	Euroagnostic	M	1942	1974	Backbencher	Edinburgh W	Scotland	Borough	1.8	Non-Signatory	Non-Signatory	Loyalist	N/A
Durant	Tony	Euroagnostic	M	1928	1974	Backbencher	Reading W	Southern England	County	25.1	Non-Signatory	Non-Signatory	Loyalist	N/A
Fairbairn	Nicholas	Euroagnostic	M	1933	1974	Backbencher	Perth and Kinross	Scotland	County	4.2	Non-Signatory	Signatory	Loyalist	N/A

Surname	Forenane	Heppell's Europe Groupings	Gender	Birth	First Entry	Position 1 May 1992 to 20 May 1993	Constituency	Region	Nature	Majority (%)	EDM-174 Signatories	EDM-549 Signatories	Maastricht Rebel?	Number of Rebellions
Hanley	Jeremy	Euroagnostic	M	1945	1983	Member of Government	Richmond & Barnes	London	Borough	8.6	Non-Signatory	Non-Signatory	Loyalist	N/A
Hannam	John	Euroagnostic	M	1929	1970	Backbencher	Exeter	Southern England	Borough	4.9	Non-Signatory	Non-Signatory	Loyalist	N/A
Howarth	Alan	Euroagnostic	M	1944	1983	Backbencher	Stratford-on-Avon	Middle England	County	33.7	Non-Signatory	Non-Signatory	Loyalist	N/A
Johnson Smith	Geoffrey	Euroagnostic	M	1924	1959	Backbencher	Wealden	Southern England	County	34.7	Non-Signatory	Non-Signatory	Loyalist	N/A
Jones	Gwilym	Euroagnostic	M	1947	1983	Member of Government	Cardiff North	Wales	Borough	6.2	Non-Signatory	Non-Signatory	Loyalist	N/A
Jopling	Michael	Euroagnostic	M	1930	1964	Backbencher	Westmorland & Lonsdale	Northern England	County	29.4	Non-Signatory	Non-Signatory	Loyalist	N/A
Knight	Greg	Euroagnostic	M	1949	1983	Member of Government	Derby N	Middle England	Borough	7.5	Non-Signatory	Non-Signatory	Loyalist	N/A
Kynoch	George	Euroagnostic	M	1946	1992	Backbencher	Kincardine & Deeside	Scotland	County	8.6	Non-Signatory	Non-Signatory	Loyalist	N/A
Lang	Ian	Euroagnostic	M	1940	1979	Member of Government	Galloway & Upper Nithsdale	Scotland	County	5.5	Non-Signatory	Non-Signatory	Loyalist	N/A
Major	John	Euroagnostic	M	1943	1979	Member of Government	Huntingdon	Southern England	County	49.3	Non-Signatory	Non-Signatory	Loyalist	N/A
Marshall	Michael, Sir	Euroagnostic	M	1930	1974	Backbencher	Arundel	Southern England	County	32.5	Non-Signatory	Non-Signatory	Loyalist	N/A
McLoughlin	Patrick	Euroagnostic	M	1957	1986	Member of Government	Derbyshire W	Middle England	County	31	Non-Signatory	Non-Signatory	Loyalist	N/A
Ottaway	Richard	Euroagnostic	M	1945	1983	Backbencher	Croydon S	London	Borough	40.7	Non-Signatory	Non-Signatory	Loyalist	N/A
Page	Richard	Euroagnostic	M	1941	1976	Backbencher	Hertfordshire SW	Southern England	County	33.9	Non-Signatory	Non-Signatory	Loyalist	N/A

Surname	Forenane	Heppell's Europe Groupings	Gender	Birth	First Entry	Position 1 May 1992 to 20 May 1993	Constituency	Region	Nature	Majority (%)	EDM-174 Signatories	EDM-549 Signatories	Maastricht Rebel?	Number of Rebellions
Patrick	Irvine	Euroagnostic	M	1929	1987	Member of Government	Sheffield Hallam	Middle England	County	12.4	Non-Signatory	Non-Signatory	Loyalist	N/A
Pattie	Geoffrey, Sir.	Euroagnostic	M	1936	1974	Backbencher	Chertsey & Walton	Southern England	County	40.2	Non-Signatory	Non-Signatory	Loyalist	N/A
Shepherd	Colin	Euroagnostic	M	1938	1974	Backbencher	Hereford	Middle England	County	6	Non-Signatory	Non-Signatory	Loyalist	N/A
Sims	Roger	Euroagnostic	M	1930	1974	Backbencher	Chislehurst	London	County	36	Non-Signatory	Non-Signatory	Loyalist	N/A
Smith	Tim	Euroagnostic	M	1947	1977	Backbencher	Beaconsfield	Southern England	County	44.6	Non-Signatory	Non-Signatory	Loyalist	N/A
Spring	Richard	Euroagnostic	M	1946	1992	Backbencher	Bury St. Edmunds	Northern England	County	30	Non-Signatory	Non-Signatory	Loyalist	N/A
Sproat	Iain	Euroagnostic	M	1938	1970	Backbencher	Harwich	Southern England	County	27.5	Non-Signatory	Non-Signatory	Loyalist	N/A
Trend	Michael	Euroagnostic	M	1952	1992	Backbencher	Windsor & Maidenhead	Southern England	County	20.5	Non-Signatory	Non-Signatory	Loyalist	N/A
Trotter	Neville	Euroagnostic	M	1932	1974	Backbencher	Tynemouth	Northern England	Borough	1	Non-Signatory	Non-Signatory	Loyalist	N/A
Viggers	Peter	Euroagnostic	M	1938	1974	Backbencher	Gosport	Southern England	Borough	30.5	Non-Signatory	Non-Signatory	Loyalist	N/A
Wheeler	John	Euroagnostic	M	1940	1979	Backbencher	Westminster N	London	Borough	8.4	Non-Signatory	Non-Signatory	Loyalist	N/A
Wolfson	Mark	Euroagnostic	M	1934	1979	Backbencher	Sevenoaks	Southern England	County	33.1	Non-Signatory	Non-Signatory	Loyalist	N/A
Wood	Timothy	Euroagnostic	M	1940	1983	Member of Government	Stevenage	Southern England	County	8.4	Non-Signatory	Non-Signatory	Loyalist	N/A
Atkins	Robert	Europhile	M	1946	1979	Member of Government	Ribble South	Northern England	County	9.2	Non-Signatory	Non-Signatory	Loyalist	N/A

Surname	Forenane	Heppell's Europe Groupings	Gender	Birth	First Entry	Position 1 May 1992 to 20 May 1993	Constituency	Region	Nature	Majority (%)	EDM-174 Signatories	EDM-549 Signatories	Maastricht Rebel?	Number of Rebellions
Atkinson	David	Europhile	M	1940	1977	Backbencher	Bournemouth E	Southern England	Borough	27.1	Non-Signatory	Non-Signatory	Loyalist	N/A
Baldry	Tony	Europhile	M	1950	1983	Member of Government	Banbury	Southern England	County	28.6	Non-Signatory	Non-Signatory	Loyalist	N/A
Batiste	Spencer	Europhile	M	1945	1983	Backbencher	Elmet	Northern England	County	5.6	Non-Signatory	Non-Signatory	Loyalist	N/A
Boswell	Tim	Europhile	M	1942	1987	Member of Government	Daventry	Southern England	County	34.1	Non-Signatory	Non-Signatory	Loyalist	N/A
Bottomley	Peter	Europhile	M	1944	1975	Backbencher	Eltham	London	Borough	4.1	Non-Signatory	Non-Signatory	Loyalist	N/A
Bottomley	Virginia	Europhile	F	1948	1984	Member of Government	Surrey SW	Southern England	County	25	Non-Signatory	Non-Signatory	Loyalist	N/A
Bright	Graham	Europhile	M	1942	1979	Backbencher	Luton S	Southern England	Borough	1.3	Non-Signatory	Non-Signatory	Loyalist	N/A
Burt	Alistair	Europhile	M	1955	1983	Member of Government	Bury N	Northern England	Borough	8.1	Non-Signatory	Non-Signatory	Loyalist	N/A
Butler	Peter	Europhile	M	1951	1992	Backbencher	Milton Keynes NE	Southern England	Borough	27.9	Non-Signatory	Non-Signatory	Loyalist	N/A
Butterfill	John	Europhile	M	1941	1983	Backbencher	Bournemouth W	Southern England	Borough	22.4	Non-Signatory	Non-Signatory	Loyalist	N/A
Carlisle	Kenneth	Europhile	M	1941	1979	Member of Government	Lincoln	Middle England	Borough	3.3	Non-Signatory	Non-Signatory	Loyalist	N/A
Chapman	Sydney	Europhile	M	1935	1979	Member of Government	Chipping Barnet	London	Borough	31.1	Non-Signatory	Non-Signatory	Loyalist	N/A
Clarke	Kenneth	Europhile	M	1940	1970	Member of Government	Rushcliffe	Middle England	County	31.2	Non-Signatory	Non-Signatory	Loyalist	N/A
Coe	Sebastian	Europhile	M	1956	1992	Backbencher	Falmouth and Camborne	Southern England	County	5.7	Non-Signatory	Non-Signatory	Loyalist	N/A

Surname	Forenane	Heppell's Europe Groupings	Gender	Birth	First Entry	Position 1 May 1992 to 20 May 1993	Constituency	Region	Nature	Majority (%)	EDM-174 Signatories	EDM-549 Signatories	Maastricht Rebel?	Number of Rebellions
Cope	John	Europhile	M	1937	1974	Member of Government	Northavon	Southern England	County	16.9	Non-Signatory	Non-Signatory	Loyalist	N/A
Cormack	Patrick	Europhile	M	1939	1970	Backbencher	Staffordshire S	Middle England	County	33.5	Non-Signatory	Non-Signatory	Loyalist	N/A
Couchman	James	Europhile	M	1942	1983	Backbencher	Gillingham	Southern England	Borough	28.8	Non-Signatory	Non-Signatory	Loyalist	N/A
Critchley	Julian, Sir	Europhile	M	1930	1959	Backbencher	Aldershot	Southern England	Borough	29.8	Non-Signatory	Non-Signatory	Loyalist	N/A
Currie	Edwina	Europhile	F	1946	1983	Backbencher	Derbyshire S	Middle England	County	6.6	Non-Signatory	Non-Signatory	Loyalist	N/A
Curry	David	Europhile	M	1944	1987	Member of Government	Skipton & Ripon	Northern England	County	31.4	Non-Signatory	Non-Signatory	Loyalist	N/A
Davies	Quentin	Europhile	M	1944	1987	Backbencher	Stamford & Spalding	Middle England	County	37.5	Non-Signatory	Non-Signatory	Loyalist	N/A
Dorrell	Stephen	Europhile	M	1952	1979	Member of Government	Loughborough	Middle England	County	18.4	Non-Signatory	Non-Signatory	Loyalist	N/A
Dykes	Hugh	Europhile	M	1939	1970	Backbencher	Harrow E	London	Borough	19.1	Non-Signatory	Non-Signatory	Loyalist	N/A
Eggar	Timothy	Europhile	M	1951	1979	Member of Government	Enfield N	London	Borough	18	Non-Signatory	Non-Signatory	Loyalist	N/A
Emery	Peter	Europhile	M	1926	1959	Backbencher	Honiton	Southern England	County	25.8	Non-Signatory	Non-Signatory	Loyalist	N/A
Evans	Jonathan	Europhile	M	1950	1992	Backbencher	Brecon & Radnor	Wales	County	0.3	Non-Signatory	Non-Signatory	Loyalist	N/A
Evans	Roger	Europhile	M	1947	1992	Backbencher	Monmouth	Wales	County	6.3	Non-Signatory	Non-Signatory	Loyalist	N/A
Fishburn	Dudley	Europhile	M	1946	1988	Backbencher	Kensington	London	Borough	11.5	Non-Signatory	Non-Signatory	Loyalist	N/A

Surname	Forenane	Heppell's Europe Groupings	Gender	Birth	First Entry	Position 1 May 1992 to 20 May 1993	Constituency	Region	Nature	Majority (%)	EDM-174 Signatories	EDM-549 Signatories	Maastricht Rebel?	Number of Rebellions
Forman	Nigel	Europhile	M	1943	1976	Member of Government	Carshalton & Wallington	London	Borough	18.8	Non-Signatory	Non-Signatory	Loyalist	N/A
Fowler	Norman	Europhile	M	1938	1970	Member of Government	Sutton Coldfield	Middle England	Borough	45.9	Non-Signatory	Non-Signatory	Loyalist	N/A
Freeman	Roger	Europhile	M	1942	1983	Member of Government	Kettering	Southern England	County	19.9	Non-Signatory	Non-Signatory	Loyalist	N/A
Garel-Jones	Tristan	Europhile	M	1941	1979	Member of Government	Watford	Southern England	Borough	16.1	Non-Signatory	Non-Signatory	Loyalist	N/A
Garnier	Edward	Europhile	M	1952	1992	Backbencher	Harborough	Middle England	County	21.6	Non-Signatory	Non-Signatory	Loyalist	N/A
Goodlad	Alastair	Europhile	M	1943	1974	Member of Government	Eddisbury	Middle England	County	20.5	Non-Signatory	Non-Signatory	Loyalist	N/A
Goodson-Wickes	Charles	Europhile	M	1945	1987	Backbencher	Wimbledon	London	Borough	29.7	Non-Signatory	Non-Signatory	Loyalist	N/A
Grant	Anthony, Sir.	Europhile	M	1925	1964	Backbencher	Cambridge-shire SW	Southern England	County	28.7	Non-Signatory	Non-Signatory	Loyalist	N/A
Gummer	John	Europhile	M	1939	1970	Member of Government	Suffolk Coastal	Southern England	County	29.8	Non-Signatory	Non-Signatory	Loyalist	N/A
Hampson	Keith	Europhile	M	1943	1974	Backbencher	Leeds NW	Northern England	Borough	15.2	Non-Signatory	Non-Signatory	Loyalist	N/A
Haselhurst	Alan	Europhile	M	1937	1970	Backbencher	Saffron Walden	Southern England	County	28	Non-Signatory	Non-Signatory	Loyalist	N/A
Heald	Oliver	Europhile	M	1954	1992	Backbencher	Hertfordshire N	Southern England	County	24.4	Non-Signatory	Non-Signatory	Loyalist	N/A
Heath	Edward	Europhile	M	1916	1950	Backbencher	Old Bexley & Sidcup	London	Borough	38.7	Non-Signatory	Non-Signatory	Loyalist	N/A
Heseltine	Michael	Europhile	M	1933	1966	Member of Government	Henley	Southern England	County	35.6	Non-Signatory	Non-Signatory	Loyalist	N/A

Surname	Forenane	Heppell's Europe Groupings	Gender	Birth	First Entry	Position 1 May 1992 to 20 May 1993	Constituency	Region	Nature	Majority (%)	EDM-174 Signatories	EDM-549 Signatories	Maastricht Rebel?	Number of Rebellions
Hicks	Robert	Europhile	M	1938	1970	Backbencher	Cornwall SE	Southern England	County	12.8	Non-Signatory	Non-Signatory	Loyalist	N/A
Higgins	Terence	Europhile	M	1928	1964	Backbencher	Worthing	Southern England	Borough	27.5	Non-Signatory	Non-Signatory	Loyalist	N/A
Hill	James	Europhile	M	1926	1970	Backbencher	Southampton Test	Southern England	Borough	1	Non-Signatory	Non-Signatory	Loyalist	N/A
Hordern	Peter	Europhile	M	1929	1964	Backbencher	Horsham	Southern England	County	36.7	Non-Signatory	Non-Signatory	Loyalist	N/A
Hughes	Robert G.	Europhile	M	1951	1987	Member of Government	Harrow W	London	Borough	32.7	Non-Signatory	Non-Signatory	Loyalist	N/A
Hunt	John	Europhile	M	1929	1964	Backbencher	Ravensbourne	London	Borough	42.4	Non-Signatory	Non-Signatory	Loyalist	N/A
Hunt	David	Europhile	M	1942	1976	Member of Government	Wirral W	Northern England	County	21.7	Non-Signatory	Non-Signatory	Loyalist	N/A
Hurd	Douglas	Europhile	M	1930	1974	Member of Government	Witney	Southern England	County	35.1	Non-Signatory	Non-Signatory	Loyalist	N/A
Jack	Michael	Europhile	M	1946	1987	Member of Government	Flyde	Southern England	County	17	Non-Signatory	Non-Signatory	Loyalist	N/A
Knight	Angela	Europhile	F	1950	1992	Backbencher	Erewash	Middle England	County	9	Non-Signatory	Non-Signatory	Loyalist	N/A
Knox	David	Europhile	M	1933	1970	Backbencher	Staffordshire Moorlands	Middle England	County	11.8	Non-Signatory	Non-Signatory	Loyalist	N/A
Lait	Jacqui	Europhile	F	1947	1992	Backbencher	Hastings & Rye	Southern England	County	12.3	Non-Signatory	Non-Signatory	Loyalist	N/A
Lester	Jim	Europhile	M	1932	1974	Backbencher	Broxtowe	Middle England	County	16.2	Non-Signatory	Non-Signatory	Loyalist	N/A
Luff	Peter	Europhile	M	1955	1992	Backbencher	Worcester	Middle England	Borough	10.2	Non-Signatory	Non-Signatory	Loyalist	N/A

Surname	Forenane	Heppell's Europe Groupings	Gender	Birth	First Entry	Position 1 May 1992 to 20 May 1993	Constituency	Region	Nature	Majority (%)	EDM-174 Signatories	EDM-549 Signatories	Maastricht Rebel?	Number of Rebellions
Lyell	Nicholas, Sir	Europhile	M	1938	1979	Member of Government	Bedfordshire Mid	Southern England	County	36.4	Non-Signatory	Non-Signatory	Loyalist	N/A
Madel	David, Sir	Europhile	M	1938	1970	Backbencher	Bedfordshire SW	Southern England	County	32.4	Non-Signatory	Non-Signatory	Loyalist	N/A
Malone	Gerry	Europhile	M	1950	1983	Backbencher	Winchester	Southern England	County	12.3	Non-Signatory	Non-Signatory	Loyalist	N/A
Mates	Michael	Europhile	M	1934	1974	Member of Government	Hampshire E	Southern England	County	39.4	Non-Signatory	Non-Signatory	Loyalist	N/A
Mayhew	Patrick	Europhile	M	1929	1974	Member of Government	Tunbridge Wells	Southern England	County	28.6	Non-Signatory	Non-Signatory	Loyalist	N/A
Mellor	David	Europhile	M	1949	1979	Member of Government	Putney	London	Borough	15.6	Non-Signatory	Non-Signatory	Loyalist	N/A
Mitchell	David	Europhile	M	1928	1964	Backbencher	Hampshire NW	Southern England	County	30.2	Non-Signatory	Non-Signatory	Loyalist	N/A
Mitchell	Andrew	Europhile	M	1956	1987	Member of Government	Gedling	Middle England	County	18.7	Non-Signatory	Non-Signatory	Loyalist	N/A
Monro	Hector, Sir.	Europhile	M	1922	1964	Member of Government	Dumfries	Scotland	County	13.1	Non-Signatory	Non-Signatory	Loyalist	N/A
Montgomery	Fergus, Sir	Europhile	M	1927	1959	Backbencher	Altrincham & Sale	Northern England	Borough	31.6	Non-Signatory	Non-Signatory	Loyalist	N/A
Moss	Malcolm	Europhile	M	1943	1987	Backbencher	Cambridge-shire NE	Southern England	County	23.8	Non-Signatory	Non-Signatory	Loyalist	N/A
Needham	Richard	Europhile	M	1942	1979	Member of Government	Wiltshire N	Southern England	County	23.4	Non-Signatory	Non-Signatory	Loyalist	N/A
Nelson	Anthony	Europhile	M	1948	1974	Backbencher	Chichester	Southern England	County	32.7	Non-Signatory	Non-Signatory	Loyalist	N/A
Newton	Tony	Europhile	M	1937	1974	Member of Government	Braintree	Southern England	County	26.6	Non-Signatory	Non-Signatory	Loyalist	N/A

Surname	Forenane	Heppell's Europe Groupings	Gender	Birth	First Entry	Position 1 May 1992 to 20 May 1993	Constituency	Region	Nature	Majority (%)	EDM-174 Signatories	EDM-549 Signatories	Maastricht Rebel?	Number of Rebellions
Nicholson	Emma	Europhile	F	1941	1987	Backbencher	Torridge & W Devon	Southern England	County	5.8	Non-Signatory	Non-Signatory	Loyalist	N/A
Onslow	Cranley	Europhile	M	1926	1964	Backbencher	Woking	Southern England	Borough	31	Non-Signatory	Non-Signatory	Loyalist	N/A
Patten	John	Europhile	M	1945	1979	Member of Government	Oxford W & Abingdon	Southern England	County	6.4	Non-Signatory	Non-Signatory	Loyalist	N/A
Pickles	Eric	Europhile	M	1952	1992	Backbencher	Brentworth & Ognar	Southern England	County	27.2	Non-Signatory	Non-Signatory	Loyalist	N/A
Powell	William	Europhile	M	1948	1983	Backbencher	Corby	Southern England	County	0.6	Non-Signatory	Non-Signatory	Loyalist	N/A
Rathbone	Tim	Europhile	M	1933	1974	Backbencher	Lewes	Southern England	County	20.1	Non-Signatory	Non-Signatory	Loyalist	N/A
Renton	Tim	Europhile	M	1932	1974	Backbencher	Sussex Mid	Southern England	County	30.6	Non-Signatory	Non-Signatory	Loyalist	N/A
Rowe	Andrew	Europhile	M	1935	1983	Backbencher	Kent Mid	Southern England	County	33.1	Non-Signatory	Non-Signatory	Loyalist	N/A
Ryder	Richard	Europhile	M	1949	1983	Member of Government	Norfolk M	Southern England	County	28.9	Non-Signatory	Non-Signatory	Loyalist	N/A
Sainsbury	Tim	Europhile	M	1932	1973	Member of Government	Hove	Southern England	Borough	24.5	Non-Signatory	Non-Signatory	Loyalist	N/A
Scott	Nicholas, Sir.	Europhile	M	1933	1966	Member of Government	Chelsea	London	Borough	47.7	Non-Signatory	Non-Signatory	Loyalist	N/A
Shaw	Giles	Europhile	M	1931	1974	Backbencher	Pudsey	Northern England	Borough	14.6	Non-Signatory	Non-Signatory	Loyalist	N/A
Soames	Nicholas, Hon.	Europhile	M	1948	1983	Member of Government	Crawley	Southern England	Borough	12.5	Non-Signatory	Non-Signatory	Loyalist	N/A
Speed	Keith	Europhile	M	1934	1968	Backbencher	Ashford	Southern England	County	30.5	Non-Signatory	Non-Signatory	Loyalist	N/A

Surname	Forenane	Heppell's Europe Groupings	Gender	Birth	First Entry	Position 1 May 1992 to 20 May 1993	Constituency	Region	Nature	Majority (%)	EDM-174 Signatories	EDM-549 Signatories	Maastricht Rebel?	Number of Rebellions
Spencer	Derek, Sir.	Europhile	M	1936	1983	Member of Government	Brighton Pavilion	Southern England	Borough	8.3	Non-Signatory	Non-Signatory	Loyalist	N/A
Spicer	James, Sir.	Europhile	M	1925	1974	Backbencher	Dorset W	Southern England	County	14.7	Non-Signatory	Non-Signatory	Loyalist	N/A
Squire	Robin	Europhile	M	1944	1979	Member of Government	Hornchurch	London	Borough	19	Non-Signatory	Non-Signatory	Loyalist	N/A
Taylor	Ian	Europhile	M	1945	1987	Backbencher	Esher	Southern England	Borough	42.8	Non-Signatory	Non-Signatory	Loyalist	N/A
Temple-Morris	Peter	Europhile	M	1938	1974	Backbencher	Leominster	Middle England	County	28.8	Non-Signatory	Non-Signatory	Loyalist	N/A
Thompson	Patrick	Europhile	M	1935	1983	Backbencher	Norwich N	Southern England	Borough	0.5	Non-Signatory	Non-Signatory	Loyalist	N/A
Thurnham	Peter	Europhile	M	1938	1983	Backbencher	Bolton NE	Northern England	Borough	0.4	Non-Signatory	Non-Signatory	Loyalist	N/A
Townsend	Cyril	Europhile	M	1937	1974	Backbencher	Bexleyheath	London	Borough	29.7	Non-Signatory	Non-Signatory	Loyalist	N/A
Ward	John	Europhile	M	1925	1979	Backbencher	Poole	Southern England	Borough	20.4	Non-Signatory	Non-Signatory	Loyalist	N/A
Whitney	Ray	Europhile	M	1930	1978	Backbencher	Wycombe	Southern England	County	30.2	Non-Signatory	Non-Signatory	Loyalist	N/A
Wiggin	Jerry	Europhile	M	1937	1969	Backbencher	Weston-super-Mare	Southern England	County	8.5	Non-Signatory	Non-Signatory	Loyalist	N/A
Yeo	Tim	Europhile	M	1945	1983	Member of Government	Suffolk S	Southern England	County	24.9	Non-Signatory	Non-Signatory	Loyalist	N/A
Young	George, Sir.	Europhile	M	1941	1974	Member of Government	Ealing Acton	London	Borough	15.7	Non-Signatory	Non-Signatory	Loyalist	N/A
Ainsworth	Peter	Eurosceptic	M	1956	1992	Backbencher	Surrey E	Southern England	County	37	Signatory	Non-Signatory	Loyalist	N/A

Surname	Forenane	Heppell's Europe Groupings	Gender	Birth	First Entry	Position 1 May 1992 to 20 May 1993	Constituency	Region	Nature	Majority (%)	EDM-174 Signatories	EDM-549 Signatories	Maastricht Rebel?	Number of Rebellions
Aitken	Jonathan	Eurosceptic	M	1942	1974	Member of Government	Thanet S	Southern England	County	23.6	Non-Signatory	Non-Signatory	Loyalist	N/A
Alexander	Richard	Eurosceptic	M	1934	1979	Backbencher	Newark	Middle England	County	14.6	Signatory	Non-Signatory	Loyalist	N/A
Allason	Rupert	Eurosceptic	M	1951	1987	Backbencher	Torbay	Southern England	Borough	10.1	Signatory	Signatory	Rebel	2
Amess	David	Eurosceptic	M	1952	1983	Backbencher	Basildon	Southern England	Borough	2.8	Non-Signatory	Non-Signatory	Loyalist	N/A
Ancram	Michael	Eurosceptic	M	1945	1974	Backbencher	Devizes	Southern England	County	26.9	Non-Signatory	Non-Signatory	Loyalist	N/A
Arbuthnot	James	Eurosceptic	M	1952	1987	Member of Government	Wanstead & Woodford	London	Borough	38.6	Non-Signatory	Non-Signatory	Loyalist	N/A
Arnold	Tom	Eurosceptic	M	1947	1974	Backbencher	Hazel Grove	Northern England	County	1.7	Signatory	Signatory	Loyalist	N/A
Arnold	Jacques	Eurosceptic	M	1947	1987	Backbencher	Gravesham	Southern England	County	9.3	Non-Signatory	Non-Signatory	Loyalist	N/A
Atkinson	Peter	Eurosceptic	M	1943	1992	Backbencher	Hexham	Northern England	County	28.2	Non-Signatory	Non-Signatory	Loyalist	N/A
Baker	Kenneth	Eurosceptic	M	1934	1968	Backbencher	Mole Valley	Southern England	County	29.1	Non-Signatory	Non-Signatory	Abstainer	N/A
Banks	Matthew	Eurosceptic	M	1961	1992	Backbencher	Southport	Southern England	Borough	5.5	Non-Signatory	Non-Signatory	Loyalist	N/A
Bellingham	Henry	Eurosceptic	M	1955	1983	Backbencher	Norfolk NW	Southern England	County	18.5	Non-Signatory	Non-Signatory	Loyalist	N/A
Bendall	Vivian	Eurosceptic	M	1938	1978	Backbencher	Ilford N	London	Borough	19.8	Signatory	Signatory	Rebel	1
Beresford	Paul, Sir.	Eurosceptic	M	1946	1992	Backbencher	Croydon C	London	Borough	24.1	Non-Signatory	Non-Signatory	Loyalist	N/A

Surname	Forename	Heppell's Europe Groupings	Gender	Birth	First Entry	Position 1 May 1992 to 20 May 1993	Constituency	Region	Nature	Majority (%)	EDM-174 Signatories	EDM-549 Signatories	Maastricht Rebel?	Number of Rebellions
Biffen	John	Eurosceptic	M	1930	1961	Ex-Minister	Shropshire N	Middle England	County	25.2	Non-Signatory	Non-Signatory	Rebel	3
Blackburn	John	Eurosceptic	M	1933	1979	Backbencher	Dudley W	Middle England	Borough	8.1	Signatory	Signatory	Loyalist	N/A
Body	Richard	Eurosceptic	M	1927	1955	Backbencher	Holland with Boston	Middle England	County	26.1	Signatory	Signatory	Rebel	3
Bonsor	Nicholas	Eurosceptic	M	1942	1979	Backbencher	Upminster	London	Borough	26.8	Signatory	Signatory	Rebel	1
Booth	Hartley	Eurosceptic	M	1946	1992	Backbencher	Finchley	London	Borough	15.5	Initial Signatory, Later Withdrawn	Non-Signatory	Loyalist	N/A
Bowden	Andrew	Eurosceptic	M	1930	1970	Backbencher	Brighton Kemptown	Southern England	Borough	7	Non-Signatory	Non-Signatory	Loyalist	N/A
Bowis	John	Eurosceptic	M	1945	1987	Backbencher	Battersea	London	Borough	9.3	Non-Signatory	Non-Signatory	Loyalist	N/A
Boyson	Rhodes, Sir	Eurosceptic	M	1925	1974	Ex-Minister	Brent North	London	Borough	24.4	Signatory	Signatory	Rebel	1
Brandreth	Gyles	Eurosceptic	M	1948	1992	Backbencher	Chester	Middle England	County	2.1	Non-Signatory	Non-Signatory	Loyalist	N/A
Brazier	Julian	Eurosceptic	M	1953	1987	Backbencher	Canterbury	Southern England	County	18.4	Non-Signatory	Non-Signatory	Loyalist	N/A
Brown	Michael	Eurosceptic	M	1951	1979	Backbencher	Brigg & Cleethorpes	Middle England	County	14.3	Non-Signatory	Non-Signatory	Loyalist	N/A
Browning	Angela	Eurosceptic	F	1946	1992	Backbencher	Tiverton	Southern England	County	18.8	Signatory	Non-Signatory	Loyalist	N/A
Budgen	Nicholas	Eurosceptic	M	1937	1974	Ex-Minister	Wolverhampton SW	Middle England	Borough	9.4	Signatory	Signatory	Rebel	3
Butcher	John	Eurosceptic	M	1946	1979	Ex-Minister	Coventry SW	Middle England	Borough	2.8	Signatory	Signatory	Rebel	2

Surname	Forenane	Heppell's Europe Groupings	Gender	Birth	First Entry	Position 1 May 1992 to 20 May 1993	Constituency	Region	Nature	Majority (%)	EDM-174 Signatories	EDM-549 Signatories	Maastricht Rebel?	Number of Rebellions
Carlisle	John	Eurosceptic	M	1942	1979	Backbencher	Luton N	Southern England	Borough	20.8	Signatory	Signatory	Rebel	3
Carrington	Matthew	Eurosceptic	M	1947	1987	Backbencher	Fulham	Northern England	Borough	42.1	Non-Signatory	Non-Signatory	Loyalist	N/A
Carttiss	Michael	Eurosceptic	M	1938	1983	Backbencher	Great Yarmouth	Southern England	County	10	Non-Signatory	Signatory	Rebel	2
Cash	Bill	Eurosceptic	M	1940	1984	Backbencher	Stafford	Middle England	County	17.6	Signatory	Signatory	Rebel	3
Churchill	Winston	Eurosceptic	M	1940	1970	Backbencher	Davyhulme	Northern England	Borough	8.8	Non-Signatory	Non-Signatory	Loyalist	N/A
Clark	Michael	Eurosceptic	M	1935	1983	Backbencher	Rochford	Southern England	County	40.8	Signatory	Signatory	Rebel	1
Clifton-Brown	Geoffrey	Eurosceptic	M	1953	1992	Backbencher	Cirencester & Tewkesbury	Southern England	County	22.2	Signatory	Non-Signatory	Loyalist	N/A
Colvin	Michael	Eurosceptic	M	1932	1979	Backbencher	Romsey & Waterside	Southern England	County	22.3	Non-Signatory	Non-Signatory	Loyalist	N/A
Congdon	David	Eurosceptic	M	1949	1992	Backbencher	Croydon NE	London	Borough	16.1	Signatory	Non-Signatory	Loyalist	N/A
Conway	Derek	Eurosceptic	M	1953	1983	Backbencher	Shrewsbury & Atcham	Middle England	County	18.8	Non-Signatory	Non-Signatory	Loyalist	N/A
Coombs	Simon	Eurosceptic	M	1947	1983	Backbencher	Swindon	Southern England	Borough	3.9	Non-Signatory	Non-Signatory	Loyalist	N/A
Coombs	Anthony	Eurosceptic	M	1952	1987	Backbencher	Wyre Forest	Middle England	County	17.1	Non-Signatory	Non-Signatory	Loyalist	N/A
Cran	James	Eurosceptic	M	1944	1987	Backbencher	Beverley	Middle England	County	25.5	Signatory	Signatory	Rebel	3
Davis	David	Eurosceptic	M	1948	1987	Member of Government	Boothferry	Middle England	County	27.2	Non-Signatory	Non-Signatory	Loyalist	N/A

Surname	Forenane	Heppell's Europe Groupings	Gender	Birth	First Entry	Position 1 May 1992 to 20 May 1993	Constituency	Region	Nature	Majority (%)	EDM-174 Signatories	EDM-549 Signatories	Maastricht Rebel?	Number of Rebellions
Day	Stephen	Eurosceptic	M	1948	1983	Backbencher	Cheadle	Northern England	Borough	28.3	Non-Signatory	Non-Signatory	Loyalist	N/A
Deva	Nirj	Eurosceptic	M	1948	1992	Backbencher	Brentford & Isleworth	London	Borough	3.9	Signatory	Signatory	Loyalist	N/A
Devlin	Tim	Eurosceptic	M	1959	1987	Backbencher	Stockton S	Northern England	Borough	5.4	Non-Signatory	Non-Signatory	Loyalist	N/A
Dickens	Geoffrey	Eurosceptic	M	1931	1979	Backbencher	Littleborough & Saddleworth	Northern England	Borough	8.4	Signatory	Non-Signatory	Loyalist	N/A
Dicks	Terry	Eurosceptic	M	1937	1983	Backbencher	Hayes & Harlington	London	Borough	0.1	Non-Signatory	Non-Signatory	Loyalist	N/A
Dover	Den	Eurosceptic	M	1938	1979	Backbencher	Chorley	Northern England	County	6.5	Signatory	Signatory	Loyalist	N/A
Duncan	Alan	Eurosceptic	M	1957	1992	Backbencher	Rutland & Melton	Middle England	County	39	Signatory	Non-Signatory	Loyalist	N/A
Duncan Smith	Iain	Eurosceptic	M	1954	1992	Backbencher	Chingford	London	Borough	34.4	Signatory	Signatory	Rebel	1
Dunn	Bob	Eurosceptic	M	1946	1979	Backbencher	Dartford	Southern England	County	17.1	Signatory	Signatory	Loyalist	N/A
Elletson	Harold	Eurosceptic	M	1960	1992	Backbencher	Blackpool North	Northern England	Borough	6.7	Non-Signatory	Non-Signatory	Loyalist	N/A
Evans	David	Eurosceptic	M	1935	1987	Backbencher	Welwyn Hatfield	Southern England	County	13.9	Initial Signatory, Later Withdrawn	Non-Signatory	Loyalist	N/A
Evans	Nigel	Eurosceptic	M	1957	1992	Backbencher	Ribble Valley	Northern England	County	11.7	Signatory	Signatory	Loyalist	N/A
Evennett	David	Eurosceptic	M	1949	1983	Backbencher	Erith & Crayford	London	Borough	5	Non-Signatory	Non-Signatory	Loyalist	N/A
Faber	David	Eurosceptic	M	1961	1992	Backbencher	Westbury	Southern England	County	17.4	Signatory	Non-Signatory	Loyalist	N/A

Surname	Forenane	Heppell's Europe Groupings	Gender	Birth	First Entry	Position 1 May 1992 to 20 May 1993	Constituency	Region	Nature	Majority (%)	EDM-174 Signatories	EDM-549 Signatories	Maastricht Rebel?	Number of Rebellions
Fabricant	Michael	Eurosceptic	M	1950	1992	Backbencher	Staffordshire M	Middle England	County	9.9	Signatory	Signatory	Loyalist	N/A
Fenner	Peggy	Eurosceptic	F	1922	1970	Backbencher	Medway	Southern England	County	17.7	Non-Signatory	Non-Signatory	Loyalist	N/A
Field	Barry	Eurosceptic	M	1946	1987	Backbencher	Isle of Wight	Southern England	County	2.3	Non-Signatory	Non-Signatory	Loyalist	N/A
Forsyth	Michael	Eurosceptic	M	1954	1983	Member of Government	Stirling	Scotland	County	1.5	Non-Signatory	Non-Signatory	Loyalist	N/A
Forth	Eric	Eurosceptic	M	1944	1983	Member of Government	Worcestershire M	Middle England	County	14.4	Non-Signatory	Non-Signatory	Loyalist	N/A
Fox	Marcus	Eurosceptic	M	1927	1970	Backbencher	Shipley	Northern England	County	21.9	Signatory	Non-Signatory	Loyalist	N/A
Fox	Liam	Eurosceptic	M	1961	1992	Backbencher	Woodspring	Southern England	County	27.1	Non-Signatory	Non-Signatory	Loyalist	N/A
French	Douglas	Eurosceptic	M	1944	1987	Backbencher	Gloucester	Southern England	Borough	9.4	Non-Signatory	Non-Signatory	Loyalist	N/A
Fry	Peter	Eurosceptic	M	1931	1969	Backbencher	Wellingborough	Southern England	County	19.5	Signatory	Signatory	Rebel	1
Gale	Roger	Eurosceptic	M	1943	1983	Backbencher	Thanet N	Southern England	County	33.7	Non-Signatory	Non-Signatory	Loyalist	N/A
Gallie	Phil	Eurosceptic	M	1939	1992	Backbencher	Ayr	Scotland	County	0.2	Signatory	Signatory	Loyalist	N/A
Gardiner	George	Eurosceptic	M	1935	1974	Backbencher	Reigate	Southern England	Borough	31.3	Signatory	Signatory	Rebel	1
Gill	Christopher	Eurosceptic	M	1936	1987	Backbencher	Ludlow	Middle England	County	25.4	Signatory	Signatory	Rebel	3
Gillan	Cheryl	Eurosceptic	F	1952	1992	Backbencher	Chesham & Amersham	Southern England	County	38.8	Signatory	Non-Signatory	Loyalist	N/A

Surname	Forenane	Heppell's Europe Groupings	Gender	Birth	First Entry	Position 1 May 1992 to 20 May 1993	Constituency	Region	Nature	Majority (%)	EDM-174 Signatories	EDM-549 Signatories	Maastricht Rebel?	Number of Rebellions
Gorman	Teresa	Eurosceptic	F	1931	1987	Backbencher	Billericay	Southern England	County	34	Signatory	Signatory	Rebel	3
Gorst	John	Eurosceptic	M	1928	1970	Backbencher	Hendon N	London	Borough	18.4	Non-Signatory	Non-Signatory	Loyalist	N/A
Greenway	Harry	Eurosceptic	M	1934	1979	Backbencher	Ealing N	London	Borough	11.9	Signatory	Signatory	Rebel	2
Greenway	John	Eurosceptic	M	1946	1987	Backbencher	Ryedale	Northern England	County	26	Signatory	Signatory	Loyalist	N/A
Griffiths	Peter	Eurosceptic	M	1928	1964	Backbencher	Portsmouth N	Southern England	Borough	22.6	Signatory	Signatory	Loyalist	N/A
Grylls	Michael	Eurosceptic	M	1934	1970	Backbencher	Surrey NW	Southern England	County	43.4	Non-Signatory	Non-Signatory	Loyalist	N/A
Hague	William	Eurosceptic	M	1961	1989	Backbencher	Richmond (Yorks)	Northern England	County	36.2	Non-Signatory	Non-Signatory	Loyalist	N/A
Hamilton	Archie	Eurosceptic	M	1941	1978	Member of Government	Epsom & Ewell	Southern England	Borough	36.7	Non-Signatory	Non-Signatory	Loyalist	N/A
Hamilton	Neil	Eurosceptic	M	1949	1983	Member of Government	Tatton	Middle England	County	27.6	Non-Signatory	Non-Signatory	Loyalist	N/A
Hargreaves	Andrew	Eurosceptic	M	1955	1987	Backbencher	Birmingham Hall Green	Middle England	Borough	7.8	Non-Signatory	Non-Signatory	Loyalist	N/A
Harris	David	Eurosceptic	M	1937	1983	Backbencher	St Ives	Southern England	County	2.9	Non-Signatory	Non-Signatory	Loyalist	N/A
Hawkins	Nick	Eurosceptic	M	1957	1992	Backbencher	Blackpool South	Northern England	Borough	3.8	Signatory	Non-Signatory	Loyalist	N/A
Hawksley	Warren	Eurosceptic	M	1943	1979	Backbencher	Halesowen & Stourbridge	Middle England	Borough	15	Signatory	Signatory	Rebel	1
Hayes	Jerry	Eurosceptic	M	1953	1983	Backbencher	Harlow	Southern England	County	5.2	Non-Signatory	Non-Signatory	Loyalist	N/A

Surname	Forenane	Heppell's Europe Groupings	Gender	Birth	First Entry	Position 1 May 1992 to 20 May 1993	Constituency	Region	Nature	Majority (%)	EDM-174 Signatories	EDM-549 Signatories	Maastricht Rebel?	Number of Rebellions
Heathcoat-Amory	David	Eurosceptic	M	1949	1983	Member of Government	Wells	Southern England	County	11.5	Non-Signatory	Non-Signatory	Loyalist	N/A
Hendry	Charles	Eurosceptic	M	1959	1992	Backbencher	High Peak	Middle England	County	8	Signatory	Non-Signatory	Loyalist	N/A
Hogg	Douglas	Eurosceptic	M	1945	1979	Member of Government	Grantham	Middle England	County	29.6	Non-Signatory	Non-Signatory	Loyalist	N/A
Horam	John	Eurosceptic	M	1939	1970	Backbencher	Orpington	London	Borough	27	Signatory	Non-Signatory	Loyalist	N/A
Howard	Michael	Eurosceptic	M	1941	1983	Member of Government	Folkestone & Hythe	London	County	16.4	Non-Signatory	Non-Signatory	Loyalist	N/A
Howell	David	Eurosceptic	M	1936	1966	Backbencher	Guildford	Southern England	County	22.1	Non-Signatory	Non-Signatory	Loyalist	N/A
Howell	Ralph	Eurosceptic	M	1923	1970	Backbencher	Norfolk N	Southern England	County	20.8	Non-Signatory	Non-Signatory	Loyalist	N/A
Hunter	Andrew	Eurosceptic	M	1943	1983	Backbencher	Basingstoke	Southern England	County	30.8	Signatory	Signatory	Rebel	1
Jackson	Robert	Eurosceptic	M	1946	1983	Member of Government	Wantage	Southern England	County	29.2	Non-Signatory	Non-Signatory	Loyalist	N/A
Jenkin	Bernard, Hon.	Eurosceptic	M	1959	1992	Backbencher	Colchester N	Southern England	Borough	24.1	Signatory	Signatory	Rebel	1
Jessel	Toby	Eurosceptic	M	1934	1970	Backbencher	Twickenham	London	Borough	10.7	Signatory	Signatory	Rebel	3
Jones	Robert	Eurosceptic	M	1950	1983	Backbencher	Hertfordshire W	Southern England	County	21.5	Signatory	Non-Signatory	Abstainer	N/A
Kellett-Bowman	Elaine	Eurosceptic	F	1924	1970	Backbencher	Lancaster	Northern England	County	6.4	Non-Signatory	Non-Signatory	Loyalist	N/A
Key	Robert	Eurosceptic	M	1945	1983	Member of Government	Salisbury	Southern England	County	14.8	Non-Signatory	Non-Signatory	Loyalist	N/A

Surname	Forename	Heppell's Europe Groupings	Gender	Birth	First Entry	Position 1 May 1992 to 20 May 1993	Constituency	Region	Nature	Majority (%)	EDM-174 Signatories	EDM-549 Signatories	Maastricht Rebel?	Number of Rebellions
King	Tom	Eurosceptic	M	1933	1970	Backbencher	Bridgwater	Southern England	County	17.1	Non-Signatory	Non-Signatory	Loyalist	N/A
Kirkhope	Timothy	Eurosceptic	M	1945	1987	Member of Government	Leeds NE	Northern England	Borough	8.6	Non-Signatory	Non-Signatory	Loyalist	N/A
Knapman	Roger	Eurosceptic	M	1944	1987	Ex-Minister	Stroud	Southern England	County	19.2	Signatory	Signatory	Rebel	2
Knight	Jill, Dame	Eurosceptic	F	1924	1966	Backbencher	Birmingham Edgbaston	Middle England	Borough	11.4	Non-Signatory	Non-Signatory	Loyalist	N/A
Lamont	Norman	Eurosceptic	M	1942	1972	Member of Government	Kingston-upon-Thames	London	Borough	25.4	Non-Signatory	Non-Signatory	Loyalist	N/A
Lawrence	Ivan	Eurosceptic	M	1936	1974	Backbencher	Burton	Middle England	County	9.7	Signatory	Signatory	Abstainer	N/A
Legg	Barry	Eurosceptic	M	1949	1992	Backbencher	Milton Keynes SW	Southern England	Borough	9.2	Signatory	Signatory	Rebel	1
Leigh	Edward	Eurosceptic	M	1950	1983	Member of Government	Gainsborough & Horncastle	Middle England	County	27.9	Non-Signatory	Non-Signatory	Loyalist	N/A
Lennox-Boyd	Mark	Eurosceptic	M	1943	1979	Member of Government	Morecambe & Lunesdale	Northern England	County	26	Non-Signatory	Non-Signatory	Loyalist	N/A
Lidington	David	Eurosceptic	M	1956	1992	Backbencher	Aylesbury	Southern England	County	29.7	Signatory	Non-Signatory	Loyalist	N/A
Lightbown	David	Eurosceptic	M	1932	1983	Member of Government	Staffordshire SE	Middle England	County	31.6	Non-Signatory	Non-Signatory	Loyalist	N/A
Lilley	Peter	Eurosceptic	M	1943	1983	Member of Government	St Albans	Northern England	County	26.5	Non-Signatory	Non-Signatory	Loyalist	N/A
Lloyd	Peter	Eurosceptic	M	1937	1979	Member of Government	Fareham	Southern England	County	36.4	Non-Signatory	Non-Signatory	Loyalist	N/A
Lord	Michael	Eurosceptic	M	1938	1983	Backbencher	Suffolk C	Southern England	County	24.1	Signatory	Signatory	Rebel	2

Surname	Forenane	Heppell's Europe Groupings	Gender	Birth	First Entry	Position 1 May 1992 to 20 May 1993	Constituency	Region	Nature	Majority (%)	EDM-174 Signatories	EDM-549 Signatories	Maastricht Rebel?	Number of Rebellions
MacGregor	John	Eurosceptic	M	1937	1974	Member of Government	Norfolk S	Southern England	County	25.6	Non-Signatory	Non-Signatory	Loyalist	N/A
MacKay	Andrew	Eurosceptic	M	1949	1977	Member of Government	Berkshire East	Southern England	County	39	Non-Signatory	Non-Signatory	Loyalist	N/A
Maclean	David	Eurosceptic	M	1953	1983	Member of Government	Penrith & the Border	Northern England	County	31.4	Non-Signatory	Non-Signatory	Loyalist	N/A
Maitland	Olga	Eurosceptic	F	1944	1992	Backbencher	Sutton & Cheam	London	Borough	21.4	Initial Signatory, Later Withdrawn	Non-Signatory	Loyalist	N/A
Mans	Keith	Eurosceptic	M	1946	1987	Backbencher	Wyre	Northern England	County	21.6	Non-Signatory	Non-Signatory	Loyalist	N/A
Marland	Paul	Eurosceptic	M	1940	1979	Backbencher	Gloucestershire W	Southern England	County	7.4	Signatory	Signatory	Loyalist	N/A
Marlow	Antony	Eurosceptic	M	1940	1979	Backbencher	Northampton N	Southern England	Borough	7.2	Signatory	Signatory	Rebel	3
Marshall	John	Eurosceptic	M	1940	1987	Backbencher	Hendon S	London	Borough	34.4	Non-Signatory	Non-Signatory	Loyalist	N/A
Martin	David	Eurosceptic	M	1945	1987	Backbencher	Portsmouth S	Southern England	Borough	0.5	Non-Signatory	Non-Signatory	Loyalist	N/A
Mawhinney	Brian	Eurosceptic	M	1940	1979	Member of Government	Peterborough	Southern England	Borough	8.2	Non-Signatory	Non-Signatory	Loyalist	N/A
McNair-Wilson	Patrick	Eurosceptic	M	1929	1964	Backbencher	New Forest	Southern England	County	33.5	Signatory	Signatory	Abstainer	N/A
Merchant	Piers	Eurosceptic	M	1951	1983	Backbencher	Beckenham	London	Borough	33	Non-Signatory	Non-Signatory	Loyalist	N/A
Mills	Iain	Eurosceptic	M	1940	1979	Backbencher	Meriden	Middle England	County	24.2	Non-Signatory	Non-Signatory	Loyalist	N/A
Moate	Roger	Eurosceptic	M	1938	1970	Backbencher	Faversham	Southern England	County	25	Signatory	Signatory	Rebel	1

Surname	Forename	Heppell's Europe Groupings	Gender	Birth	First Entry	Position 1 May 1992 to 20 May 1993	Constituency	Region	Nature	Majority (%)	EDM-174 Signatories	EDM-549 Signatories	Maastricht Rebel?	Number of Rebellions
Neubert	Michael	Eurosceptic	M	1933	1974	Backbencher	Romford	London	Borough	27.1	Non-Signatory	Signatory	Loyalist	N/A
Nicholls	Patrick	Eurosceptic	M	1948	1983	Backbencher	Teignbridge	Southern England	County	14.2	Non-Signatory	Non-Signatory	Loyalist	N/A
Nicholson	David	Eurosceptic	M	1944	1987	Backbencher	Taunton	Southern England	County	5.2	Non-Signatory	Non-Signatory	Loyalist	N/A
Norris	Steven	Eurosceptic	M	1945	1983	Member of Government	Epping Forest	Southern England	County	37.1	Non-Signatory	Non-Signatory	Loyalist	N/A
Oppenheim	Phillip, Hon.	Eurosceptic	M	1956	1983	Backbencher	Amber Valley	Middle England	County	1.2	Non-Signatory	Non-Signatory	Loyalist	N/A
Paice	James	Eurosceptic	M	1949	1987	Backbencher	Cambridge-shire SE	Southern England	County	37.6	Non-Signatory	Non-Signatory	Loyalist	N/A
Pawsey	Jim	Eurosceptic	M	1933	1979	Backbencher	Rugby & Kenilworth	Middle England	County	20.3	Signatory	Signatory	Rebel	1
Peacock	Elizabeth	Eurosceptic	F	1937	1983	Backbencher	Batley & Spen	Northern England	County	2.3	Non-Signatory	Non-Signatory	Loyalist	N/A
Porter	David	Eurosceptic	M	1948	1987	Backbencher	Waveney	Southern England	County	9.7	Signatory	Signatory	Rebel	3
Porter	Barry	Eurosceptic	M	1939	1979	Backbencher	Wirral S	Northern England	County	16.3	Signatory	Signatory	Loyalist	N/A
Portillo	Michael	Eurosceptic	M	1953	1984	Member of Government	Enfield Southgate	London	Borough	31.7	Non-Signatory	Non-Signatory	Loyalist	N/A
Redwood	John	Eurosceptic	M	1951	1987	Member of Government	Wokingham	Southern England	County	36.3	Non-Signatory	Non-Signatory	Loyalist	N/A
Richards	Rod	Eurosceptic	M	1947	1992	Backbencher	Clwyd NW	Wales	County	11.4	Non-Signatory	Non-Signatory	Loyalist	N/A
Riddick	Graham	Eurosceptic	M	1955	1987	Backbencher	Colne Valley	Northern England	County	12.2	Non-Signatory	Non-Signatory	Loyalist	N/A

Surname	Forenane	Heppell's Europe Groupings	Gender	Birth	First Entry	Position 1 May 1992 to 20 May 1993	Constituency	Region	Nature	Majority (%)	EDM-174 Signatories	EDM-549 Signatories	Maastricht Rebel?	Number of Rebellions
Rifkind	Malcolm	Eurosceptic	M	1946	1974	Member of Government	Edinburgh Pentlands	Scotland	Borough	9.6	Non-Signatory	Non-Signatory	Loyalist	N/A
Robathan	Andrew	Eurosceptic	M	1951	1992	Backbencher	Blaby	Middle England	County	37.2	Signatory	Signatory	Rebel	1
Roberts	Wyn, Sir.	Eurosceptic	M	1930	1970	Member of Government	Conwy	Wales	County	2.4	Non-Signatory	Non-Signatory	Loyalist	N/A
Robertson	Raymond	Eurosceptic	M	1959	1992	Backbencher	Aberdeen South	Scotland	Borough	3.7	Signatory	Non-Signatory	Loyalist	N/A
Robinson	Mark	Eurosceptic	M	1946	1983	Backbencher	Somerton & Frome	Southern England	County	7.4	Non-Signatory	Non-Signatory	Loyalist	N/A
Roe	Marion	Eurosceptic	F	1936	1983	Backbencher	Broxbourne	Southern England	Borough	41.6	Signatory	Signatory	Loyalist	N/A
Rumbold	Angela	Eurosceptic	F	1932	1982	Backbencher	Mitcham & Morden	London	Borough	3.4	Non-Signatory	Non-Signatory	Loyalist	N/A
Sackville	Tom, Hon.	Eurosceptic	M	1950	1983	Member of Government	Bolton W	Northern England	County	1.8	Non-Signatory	Non-Signatory	Loyalist	N/A
Shaw	David	Eurosceptic	M	1950	1987	Backbencher	Dover	Southern England	County	1.4	Signatory	Signatory	Loyalist	N/A
Shepherd	Gillian	Eurosceptic	F	1940	1987	Member of Government	Norfolk SW	Southern England	County	27.5	Non-Signatory	Non-Signatory	Loyalist	N/A
Shepherd	Richard	Eurosceptic	M	1942	1979	Backbencher	Aldridge-Brownhills	Middle England	Borough	21.1	Signatory	Signatory	Rebel	3
Shersby	Michael	Eurosceptic	M	1933	1972	Backbencher	Uxbridge	London	Borough	27.1	Signatory	Non-Signatory	Loyalist	N/A
Skeet	Trevor, Sir	Eurosceptic	M	1918	1959	Backbencher	Bedfordshire North	Southern England	County	19.7	Signatory	Signatory	Rebel	3
Smith	Dudley	Eurosceptic	M	1926	1959	Backbencher	Warwick & Leamington	Middle England	Borough	15.4	Non-Signatory	Non-Signatory	Loyalist	N/A

Surname	Forenane	Heppell's Europe Groupings	Gender	Birth	First Entry	Position 1 May 1992 to 20 May 1993	Constituency	Region	Nature	Majority (%)	EDM-174 Signatories	EDM-549 Signatories	Maastricht Rebel?	Number of Rebellions
Spicer	Michael	Eurosceptic	M	1943	1974	Ex-Minister	Worcestershire S	Middle England	County	25.1	Signatory	Signatory	Rebel	3
Spink	Bob, Dr.	Eurosceptic	M	1948	1992	Backbencher	Castle Point	Southern England	Borough	31.6	Non-Signatory	Non-Signatory	Loyalist	N/A
Stanley	John	Eurosceptic	M	1942	1974	Backbencher	Tonbridge & Malling	Southern England	County	33.7	Non-Signatory	Non-Signatory	Loyalist	N/A
Steen	Anthony	Eurosceptic	M	1939	1974	Backbencher	S Hams	Southern England	County	20.4	Signatory	Non-Signatory	Loyalist	N/A
Stephen	Michael	Eurosceptic	M	1942	1992	Backbencher	Shoreham	Southern England	County	24.7	Non-Signatory	Non-Signatory	Loyalist	N/A
Stern	Michael	Eurosceptic	M	1942	1983	Backbencher	Bristol NW	Southern England	Borough	0.1	Signatory	Non-Signatory	Loyalist	N/A
Stewart	Allan	Eurosceptic	M	1942	1979	Member of Government	Eastwood	Middle England	County	22.7	Non-Signatory	Non-Signatory	Loyalist	N/A
Streeter	Gary	Eurosceptic	M	1955	1992	Backbencher	Plymouth Sutton	Southern England	Borough	21.8	Non-Signatory	Non-Signatory	Loyalist	N/A
Sumberg	David	Eurosceptic	M	1941	1983	Backbencher	Bury S	Northern England	Borough	1.5	Non-Signatory	Non-Signatory	Loyalist	N/A
Sweeney	Walter	Eurosceptic	M	1949	1992	Backbencher	Vale of Glamorgan	Wales	County	0	Non-Signatory	Signatory	Rebel	1
Sykes	John	Eurosceptic	M	1956	1992	Backbencher	Scarborough	Northern England	County	19.9	Signatory	Signatory	Loyalist	N/A
Tapsell	Peter, Sir.	Eurosceptic	M	1930	1959	Backbencher	East Lindsey	Middle England	County	19	Non-Signatory	Signatory	Rebel	2
Taylor	John	Eurosceptic	M	1941	1983	Backbencher	Solihull	Middle England	Borough	39.9	Non-Signatory	Non-Signatory	Loyalist	N/A
Taylor	Teddy	Eurosceptic	M	1937	1964	Ex-Minister	Southend E	Southern England	Borough	31.3	Signatory	Signatory	Rebel	3

Surname	Forenane	Heppell's Europe Groupings	Gender	Birth	First Entry	Position 1 May 1992 to 20 May 1993	Constituency	Region	Nature	Majority (%)	EDM-174 Signatories	EDM-549 Signatories	Maastricht Rebel?	Number of Rebellions
Thomason	Roy	Eurosceptic	M	1944	1992	Backbencher	Bromsgrove	Middle England	County	23.4	Signatory	Non-Signatory	Loyalist	N/A
Thompson	Donald, Sir.	Eurosceptic	M	1931	1979	Backbencher	Calder Valley	Northern England	County	8	Non-Signatory	Non-Signatory	Loyalist	N/A
Thornton	Malcolm	Eurosceptic	M	1939	1979	Backbencher	Crosby	Northern England	Borough	21.8	Non-Signatory	Non-Signatory	Loyalist	N/A
Townend	John	Eurosceptic	M	1934	1979	Backbencher	Bridlington	Middle England	County	24.7	Signatory	Signatory	Rebel	1
Tracey	Richard	Eurosceptic	M	1943	1983	Backbencher	Surbiton	London	Borough	27.6	Non-Signatory	Non-Signatory	Loyalist	N/A
Tredinnick	David	Eurosceptic	M	1950	1987	Backbencher	Bosworth	Middle England	County	28.3	Non-Signatory	Non-Signatory	Loyalist	N/A
Twinn	Ian, Dr.	Eurosceptic	M	1950	1983	Backbencher	Edmonton	London	Borough	1.2	Non-Signatory	Non-Signatory	Loyalist	N/A
Vaughan	Gerard	Eurosceptic	M	1923	1970	Backbencher	Reading E	Southern England	Borough	26.9	Signatory	Signatory	Abstainer	N/A
Waldegrave	William, Hon.	Eurosceptic	M	1946	1979	Member of Government	Bristol W	Southern England	Borough	11.6	Non-Signatory	Non-Signatory	Loyalist	N/A
Walden	George	Eurosceptic	M	1939	1983	Backbencher	Buckingham	Southern England	County	41.6	Non-Signatory	Non-Signatory	Loyalist	N/A
Walker	Bill	Eurosceptic	M	1929	1979	Ex-Minister	Tayside N	Scotland	County	9.2	Signatory	Signatory	Rebel	2
Waller	Gary	Eurosceptic	M	1945	1979	Backbencher	Keighley	Northern England	County	6.6	Non-Signatory	Signatory	Loyalist	N/A
Wardle	Charles	Eurosceptic	M	1939	1983	Member of Government	Bexhill & Battle	Southern England	County	31.4	Non-Signatory	Non-Signatory	Loyalist	N/A
Waterson	Nigel	Eurosceptic	M	1950	1992	Backbencher	Eastbourne	Southern England	Borough	8.9	Signatory	Non-Signatory	Loyalist	N/A

Surname	Forenane	Heppell's Europe Groupings	Gender	Birth	First Entry	Position 1 May 1992 to 20 May 1993	Constituency	Region	Nature	Majority (%)	EDM-174 Signatories	EDM-549 Signatories	Maastricht Rebel?	Number of Rebellions
Watts	John	Eurosceptic	M	1947	1983	Backbencher	Slough	Southern England	Borough	0.9	Signatory	Non-Signatory	Loyalist	N/A
Wells	Bowen	Eurosceptic	M	1935	1979	Backbencher	Hertford & Stortford	Southern England	County	32.5	Non-Signatory	Non-Signatory	Loyalist	N/A
Whittingdale	John	Eurosceptic	M	1959	1992	Backbencher	S Colchester & Maldon	Southern England	County	31.9	Signatory	Signatory	Rebel	1
Widdecombe	Ann	Eurosceptic	F	1947	1987	Member of Government	Maidstone	Southern England	County	27.9	Non-Signatory	Non-Signatory	Loyalist	N/A
Wilkinson	John	Eurosceptic	M	1940	1970	Backbencher	Ruislip-Northwood	London	Borough	44.6	Signatory	Signatory	Rebel	2
Willetts	David	Eurosceptic	M	1956	1992	Backbencher	Havant	Southern England	Borough	30	Signatory	Non-Signatory	Loyalist	N/A
Wilshire	David	Eurosceptic	M	1943	1987	Backbencher	Spelthorne	Southern England	Borough	35.6	Signatory	Non-Signatory	Loyalist	N/A
Winterton	Ann	Eurosceptic	F	1941	1983	Backbencher	Congleton	Middle England	County	18.7	Signatory	Signatory	Rebel	3
Winterton	Nicholas	Eurosceptic	M	1938	1971	Backbencher	Macclesfield	Middle England	County	36.1	Signatory	Signatory	Rebel	3
Adley	Robert	Insufficient Data	M	1935	1970	Backbencher	Christchurch	Southern England	County	39.9	Non-Signatory	Non-Signatory	Loyalist	N/A
Chaplin	Judith	Insufficient Data	F	1939	1992	Backbencher	Newbury	Southern England	County	18.6	Non-Signatory	Non-Signatory	Loyalist	N/A
Fookes	Janet	Insufficient Data	F	1936	1970	Backbencher	Plymouth Drake	Southern England	Borough	5.2	Non-Signatory	Non-Signatory	Loyalist	N/A
Milligan	Stephen	Insufficient Data	M	1948	1992	Backbencher	Eastleigh	Southern England	Borough	23.3	Non-Signatory	Non-Signatory	Loyalist	N/A
Morris	Michael	Insufficient Data	M	1936	1974	Backbencher	Northampton S	Southern England	Borough	25.5	Non-Signatory	Non-Signatory	Loyalist	N/A

Bibliography

Primary Sources

Published Editions of Documents

http://hansard.millbanksystems.com/commons/1992/may/21/european-communities-amendment-bill [accessed 31 January 2014].

http://hansard.millbanksystems.com/commons/1992/nov/04/european-communities-amendment-bill [accessed 31 January 2014].

http://hansard.millbanksystems.com/commons/1993/may/20/european-communities-amendment-bill [accessed 31 January 2014].

http://hansard.millbanksystems.com/commons/1991/dec/19/maastricht [accessed 5 May 2014].

http://hansard.millbanksystems.com/commons/1971/oct/28/european-communities [accessed 31 January 2014].

Guardian.

Huffington Post.

Independent.

The Times.

Contemporary Published Documents

Dod's Parliamentary Companion 1993 (Etchingham, 1993).

Butler, D. and G. (eds.), *British Political Facts* (London, 2011).

Rallings C. and Trasher M. (eds.), *British Parliamentary Election Results 1983-1997* (Aldershot, 1999).

Memoirs and Autobiographies

Boyson, R., *Speaking My Mind* (London, 1995).

Brandreth, G., *Breaking the Code: Westminster Diaries May 1990-May 1997* (London, 1999).

Fowler, N., *A Political Suicide: The Conservatives' Voyage into the Wilderness* (London, 2008).

Gardiner, G., *A Bastard's Tale* (London, 1999).

Gill, C., *Whip's Nightmare: Diary of a Maastricht Rebel* (Spennymoor, 2003).

Gorman, T., *The Bastards: Dirty Tricks and the Challenge to Europe* (London, 1993).

Heath, E., *The Course of My Life: My Autobiography* (St. Ives, 1998).

Heseltine, M., *Life in the Jungle: My Autobiography* (London, 2000).

Heathcoat-Amory, D., *Confessions of a Eurosceptic* (Croydon, 2012).

Hogg, S. and Hill, J., *Too Close to Call: Power and Politics - John Major in No. 10* (St. Ives, 1995).

Knight, J., *About the House* (London, 1995).

Lamont, N., *In Office* (London, 1999).

Lamont, N., *Sovereign Britain* (London, 1995).

Lang, I., *Blue Remembered Years: A Political Memoir* (London, 2002).

Major, J., *The Autobiography* (St. Ives, 1999).

Renton, T., *The Chief Whip: People, Power and Patronage in Westminster* (Croydon, 2005).

Redwood, R., *Singing the Blues: The Once and Future Conservatives* (London, 2004).

Ridley, N., *My Style of Government: The Thatcher Years* (London, 1992).

Spicer, M., *The Spicer Diaries* (London, 2012).

Taylor, E., *Teddy Boy Blue* (Glasgow, 2008).

Thatcher, M., *The Path to Power* (London, 1995).

Williams, H., *Guilty Men: Conservative Decline and Fall, 1992-1997* (London, 1998).

Interviews

Cash, W., 17 December 2013, Palace of Westminster, London.

Legg, B., 20 December 2013, Churchill Gardens, London.

Lilley, P., 21 January 2014, Palace of Westminster, London.

Redwood, J., 10 December 2013, Portcullis House, London.

Secondary Sources

Books

Bale, T., *The Conservative Party: From Thatcher to Cameron* (Cambridge, 2010).

Buller, J., *National Statecraft and European Integration: The Conservative Government and the European Union 1979-1997* (London, 2000).

Crowson, N. J., *The Conservative Party and European Integration Since 1945: At the heart of Europe?* (Abingdon, 2007).

Crick, M., *In Search of Michael Howard* (London, 2005).

Dorey, P. (ed.), *The Major Premiership 1990-1997* (Basingstoke, 1999).

Gove, M., *Michael Portillo: The Future of the Right* (London, 1995).

Heffer, S., *Like the Roman: The Life of Enoch Powell* (London, 1999).

Lynch, P., *The Politics of Nationhood: Sovereignity, Britishness and Conservative Politics* (Chippenham, 1999).

Patterson, B., *The Conservative Party and Europe* (London, 2011).

Seldon, A., *Major: A Political Life* (Guernsey, 1997).

Stephens, P., *Politics and the Pound: The Tories, the Economy and Europe* (London, 1997).

Thompson, H., *The British Conservative Government and the European Exchange Rate Mechanism 1979-1994* (New York, 1996).

Turner, J., *The Tories and Europe* (Manchester, 2000).

Whiteley, P., Seyd, P. and Richardson, J., *True Blues: The Politics of Conservative Party Membership* (Oxford, 1994).

Young, H., *This Blessed Plot: Britain and Europe from Churchill to Blair* (London, 1998).

Young, J. W., *Britain and European Unity, 1945-1999* (Basignstoke,2000).

Articles and Essays

Alderman, K., 'The Conservative Party Leadership Election of 1995', *Parliamentary Affairs*, 49, no. 2 (1996), pp. 316-332.

Baker, D., Fountain, I., etc., 'Backbench Conservative attitudes towards European integration', *Political Quarterly*, 66, no. 2 (1995).

Baker, D., Gamble, A. and Ludlam, S., 'Whips or Scorpions? The Maastricht Vote and the Conservative Party', *Parliamentary Affairs*, 46, no. 2 (1993), pp. 151-166.

Baker, D., Gamble, A., and Ludlum, S., 'The Parliamentary Siege of Maastricht 1993: Conservative Divisions and British Ratification', *Parliamentary Affairs*, 47, no. 1 (1994), pp. 37-60.

Baker, D., Gamble, A. and Ludlam, S., 'More Classless and Less Thatcherite: Conservative Ministers and New Conservative MPs. After the 1992 Election', *Parliamentary Affairs*, 45, no. 4 (1992), pp. 656-668.

Baker, D., Gamble, A., etc., '1846,1906,1996? Conservative splits and European integration', *Political Quarterly*, 64, no. 4 (1993).

Berrington, H. and Hague, R., 'Europe, Thatcherism and Traditionalism: Opinion, Rebellion and the Maastricht Treaty in the Backbench Conservative Party, 1992-1994', *West European Politics*, 21, no. 1 (1998), pp. 44-71.

Cowley, P. and Garry, J., 'The British Conservative Party and Europe: The Choosing of John Major', *British Journal of Political Science*, 28, no. 3 (1998), pp. 473-499.

Evans, G., 'Euroscepticism and Conservative Electoral Support: How an Asset Became a Liability', *British Journal of Political Science*, 28, no. 4 (1998), pp. 573-590.

Forster, A., 'Anti-Europeans, Anti-Marketeers and Eurosceptics: The Evolution and Influence of Labour and Conservative Opposition to Europe', *The Political Quarterly*, 73, no. 3 (2002), pp. 299-308.

Garry, J., 'The British Conservative Party: Divisions Over European Policy', *West European Politics*, 18, no. 4 (1995), pp. 170-189.

Heppell, T., 'The ideological composition of the Parliamentary Conservative Party 1992-97', *British Journal of Politics and International Relations*, 4, no. 2 (2002), pp. 299-324.

Jones, P. and Hudson, J., 'The Quality of Political Leadership: A Case Study of John Major', *British Journal of Political Science*, 26, no. 2 (1996), pp. 229-244.

Kaiser, W., 'Using Europe and abusing the Europeans: the Conservatives and the European Community 1957-1994', *Contemporary Record*, 8, no. 2 (1994).

Kellner, P., 'Why the Tories were Trounced', *Parliamentary Affairs*, 50, no. 4 (1997), pp. 616-630.

McAllister, I. and Studlar, D., 'Conservative Euroscepticism and the Referendum Party in the 1997 British General Election', *Party Politics*, 6, no. 3 (2000), pp. 359-371.

Sowemimo, M., 'The Conservative Party and European integration 1988-1995', *Party Politics*, 2, no. 1 (1996).

Miscellaneous

http://www.electoralcalculus.co.uk/regional_defns.html [accessed 31 January 2014].